CAMBRIDGE LIBRARY COLLECTION

Books of enduring scholarly value

Women's Writing

The later twentieth century saw a huge wave of academic interest in women's writing, which led to the rediscovery of neglected works from a wide range of genres, periods and languages. Many books that were immensely popular and influential in their own day are now studied again, both for their own sake and for what they reveal about the social, political and cultural conditions of their time. A pioneering resource in this area is Orlando: Women's Writing in the British Isles from the Beginnings to the Present (http://orlando.cambridge.org), which provides entries on authors' lives and writing careers, contextual material, timelines, sets of internal links, and bibliographies. Its editors have made a major contribution to the selection of the works reissued in this series within the Cambridge Library Collection, which focuses on non-fiction publications by women on a wide range of subjects from astronomy to biography, music to political economy, and education to prison reform.

Observations on the Natural Claim of the Mother to the Custody of her Infant Children

Caroline Norton (1808–77), author and law reform campaigner, was the granddaughter of the playwright Sheridan and soprano Elizabeth Linley. Her disastrous, violent marriage in 1827 to the financially irresponsible Tory M.P. and barrister George Norton led her to seek escape in writing poetry. Anonymous autobiographical novels followed, exploring women's powerlessness in marriage, together with regular contributions to periodicals such as *Macmillan's Magazine*. Flamboyant, intelligent and temperamental, she secured her place in literary society, numbering Disraeli and Dickens among her friends. Ever jealous, her husband accused her of adultery with Lord Melbourne, but the case was unproven. In revenge, he refused his wife access to their sons, and it was this act which led to her determined campaign to improve the rights of women in marriage and divorce. This work, first published anonymously in 1837, was instrumental in the subsequent passing of the Custody of Infants Act (1839).

Cambridge University Press has long been a pioneer in the reissuing of out-of-print titles from its own backlist, producing digital reprints of books that are still sought after by scholars and students but could not be reprinted economically using traditional technology. The Cambridge Library Collection extends this activity to a wider range of books which are still of importance to researchers and professionals, either for the source material they contain, or as landmarks in the history of their academic discipline.

Drawing from the world-renowned collections in the Cambridge University Library and other partner libraries, and guided by the advice of experts in each subject area, Cambridge University Press is using state-of-the-art scanning machines in its own Printing House to capture the content of each book selected for inclusion. The files are processed to give a consistently clear, crisp image, and the books finished to the high quality standard for which the Press is recognised around the world. The latest print-on-demand technology ensures that the books will remain available indefinitely, and that orders for single or multiple copies can quickly be supplied.

The Cambridge Library Collection brings back to life books of enduring scholarly value (including out-of-copyright works originally issued by other publishers) across a wide range of disciplines in the humanities and social sciences and in science and technology.

Observations on the Natural Claim of the Mother to the Custody of her Infant Children

As Affected by the
Common Law Right of the Father

Caroline Sheridan Norton

CAMBRIDGE
UNIVERSITY PRESS

CAMBRIDGE UNIVERSITY PRESS

Cambridge, New York, Melbourne, Madrid, Cape Town,
Singapore, São Paolo, Delhi, Mexico City

Published in the United States of America by Cambridge University Press, New York

www.cambridge.org
Information on this title: www.cambridge.org/9781108040341

© in this compilation Cambridge University Press 2013

This edition first published 1837
This digitally printed version 2013

ISBN 978-1-108-04034-1 Paperback

OBSERVATIONS

ON THE

NATURAL CLAIM OF THE MOTHER

TO THE

CUSTODY OF HER INFANT CHILDREN,

AS AFFECTED BY THE

Common Law Right of the Father.

ILLUSTRATED BY CASES OF PECULIAR HARDSHIP.

LONDON:

JAMES RIDGWAY AND SONS, PICCADILLY.

MDCCCXXXVII.

OBSERVATIONS,

&c. &c.

AT the time Mr. Wellesley's case was before the public, great interest was excited, and several publications issued from the press, explanatory of the power of the Court of Chancery to control the right of a father to the custody of his children. The observations then published, and the cases quoted in support of them, tend to shew, that so sacred and indefeasible is the father's right held by the English law, that there are scarcely *any* instances in which the Court has thought fit to interfere, or remove children from the custody of their natural guardian and protector.

Incidentally, it is also shewn, that in cases of dispute and separation between man and wife, the claim of the mother is not only subordinate to that of the father, but is totally disregarded, or rather, has no acknowledged existence in law. Numerous cases exist, in which the women have attempted to establish a claim to the custody of their children, but the result has invariably been *against the mother*, except in one or two rare instances, where property was affected ; for the sake of the security of which property, and not from any admission of the mother's natural claim, the decisions were made against the father.

In cases where property was not affected, I cannot find that any instance has occurred in which the bad character of the father, *even though he should have forsaken his wife, and be living in adultery*, has operated on the decisions of the Courts of Law as to the mother's claim, those decisions being founded on what is termed " the common law-right of the father" to the custody of his child ; and though in almost all the cases reported, both counsel and judge admit the severity and injustice of the law as affecting the mother, it does not appear that any attempt has ever been made to revise or alter it.

It is a common error among women to suppose that every mother has a *right* to the custody of her child till it attain the age of seven years. By a curious anomaly in law, the mother of a *bastard child* HAS *this right*, while the mothers of legitimate children are excluded from it,—the law as regards children born in wedlock being as follows : (*vide the cases which follow the remarks*).

The father has a right over his child *from the hour of its birth*, and may, if he so pleases, enter by force or stratagem the house where his wife shall have taken refuge, seize the infant at her very breast, and deliver it over to the care and nurture of strangers.

He may forsake his wife for a mistress, and avow his intention of persisting to keep that mistress, and yet may by law claim from his wife her *infant female children*, and should she resist his claim, she is subject to imprisonment for contempt of Court.

The child may be *diseased and dying*, and it may be proved that this was the sole reason for the mother endeavouring to retain possession of it, but the Court of Law will take it from the custody of the mother, *and deliver it over to any stranger the father may choose to appoint.*

He may deny all access to the children, remove them from place to place, *with a view to prevent the mother from even obtaining intelligence of their welfare;* give them into the care of utter strangers, and forbid those strangers to afford any clue to the place of abode of the children; and the Courts of Law cannot even make an order that the mother shall have *access to her children*, or *see them.*

It is to observations on the nature and extent of this unacknowledged claim of the mother, that I would more particularly address myself at the present time; and in order to do so more effectually, I have selected cases in support of the above brief explanation of the unlimited power accorded to the father, with the intention of proving, *that such power has in many instances been most grossly and savagely abused ;* that *it has been exercised in the extremest spirit of vengeance and cruelty ;* that *it is productive of injury to the child, of suffering to the mother;* and *has a direct tendency against the moral order and well-being of society.*

I have given the cases as familiarly as possible, my object not being to argue against the technicalities of law, but against the principle on which it rests ; and I apprehend, that no right-minded man can read through the examples here given, without admitting the necessity of some such alteration in that law, as shall afford a reasonable protection to the weak and helpless of the other sex, under circumstances of great grievance and oppression.

It may be as well to observe, that neither the remarks which precede these cases, nor those which follow them, are intended to apply to instances in which the woman shall have left her house for the protection of a lover ; in that case she may be fairly supposed to have balanced the affection and society of her children against that for which she has forsaken them, and to *know* that her intercourse with them depends on the mercy of their father. It is only in cases of separation for other causes, that I would argue, that the wife *should at least be put on a footing with the mother of an illegitimate child, and retain the*

custody of children under the age of nurture
(held to be seven years); *and that after they
have passed such age,*—though the father might
have power to remove them from the custody of
the mother, to the care of such persons as he
might choose to conduct their education,—*he
should* NOT *have power to forbid access to the
children at convenient seasons, unless he could
prove sufficient grounds for such refusal.* In
short, that the woman should have some tribunal
to appeal to, beyond the caprice of an angry
man.

I shall here leave the subject for the present,
and proceed to some of the examples of that
abuse of " the father's right," which to my mind
forms a stronger plea than any argument, that
such a power ought not to exist.

———————

* CASE OF MRS. DE MANNEVILLE, A. D. 1804.

This is a case well known, and perpetually
quoted as a precedent to support other decisions
of a like nature, though it may fairly be doubted
whether the original decision should ever have
been made.

———————

* See East's Reports, vol. v. page 221, and Vesey's Reports,
vol. x. page 61.

In 1800, Margaret Compton, an English-woman, possessed of property to the amount of 700*l.* a year, married Lenard de Manneville, a French emigrant. By a settlement previous to the marriage, this property was vested in trustees for her separate use for life, and after her death, and in case of her husband surviving her, the interest of 2000*l.* was to be paid to him for his life.

The settlement also contained a covenant, that he should in no way compel his wife, after marriage, to live in France, or in any other country than Great Britain.

Mr. de Manneville seems to have been discontented with the pecuniary arrangements made by his wife, for it appeared when the case came before the courts of law, that he had harassed and persecuted her, to compel her to execute a will in his favour, that in defiance of the covenant he had threatened to carry her by main force out of the kingdom, and afterwards, in 1804, on her becoming a mother, he had in like manner threatened to carry the child away.

Mrs. de Manneville, fearing that he would put his threats in execution, withdrew from his house at Bolton in Lancashire, to the house of a friend of her mother's near Bolton, taking with her the baby (whom she was nursing), but leaving a note informing him where he might see the child. Being soon afterwards advised, from the state of her health, to

send the baby to a nurse for a few days, her husband took that opportunity of getting possession
of it, but being taken into custody under the alien
act, two women, who had been sent by the mother
to take care of the child, brought it back to her.
Mrs. de Manneville, meanwhile, went to reside
under the protection of her own mother, Mrs.
Compton, and on the night of the 10th of April,
her husband found means, *by force and stratagem,*
to get into the house where she was ; seized the
child, *then at the breast,* and carried it away
almost naked in an open carriage in inclement
weather.

Mrs. de Manneville applied to the King's
Bench for a writ of *habeas corpus,* directing her
husband to produce her infant daughter, and
made affidavit of the circumstances under which
it had been seized and violently torn from her,—
and also that she had separated herself from her
husband on account of his cruelty and ill-usage ;
and feared the removal of the child to France.

The case was argued ; and it appearing that
there was no clear ground for supposing that Mr.
de Manneville intended to remove the child out
of the kingdom beyond the vague fears of the
mother, Lord Ellenborough decided that the
father was the person entitled *by law* to the custody of the child; and on its being urged that
the infant was of very tender age, that its removal
from the mother deprived it of its accustomed

proper nutriment, and that the father had obtained possession of it by force and fraud, Lord
Ellenborough further remarked, that there was no
pretence that the child had been injured for want
of nurture,; that the father had a *legal right*, had
not abused that right, and was entitled to have
the child restored to him.

The application to the Court of King's Bench
having failed, a petition was presented to the
Court of Chancery (in the cause which had been
instituted for the purpose of having the trusts
executed and the property secured). The prayer
of the petition was, that the infant be produced
in court, and *delivered over to* ITS MOTHER; and in
case the court should be of opinion that the
infant should not be taken from THE FATHER, then
that he be restrained from carrying away either
the mother or child out of the jurisdiction of the
Court.

In these proceedings, as well as in the former
attempt on the part of the mother to regain her
child, the main point considered by the Court was
solely whether Mr. de Manneville, being an alien,
and native of a country then at war with England,
did or did not intend to take this infant, a natural
born subject of Great Britain, out of the kingdom;
and it was also the only point with reference to
which the decision was made; for it appearing on
further evidence that the mother *was* justified in
fearing the removal of the child, and that the

probability was, that such removal would take
place unless prevented,—an order was made re-
straining Mr. de Manneville from taking the
infant out of the jurisdiction of the Court. There
was, as I have said, no reference to the mother's
claim in this decision, nor was such claim in any
way admitted; on the contrary, it was observed
in the course of this case, " *the law is clear that
the custody of a child, of whatever age, belongs to
the father;*" and although Lord Eldon mentioned
instances of interference on the part of the Court,
yet neither had these instances any reference to
the mother's claim; and it was established on that
case that " the father's right " extends to the
hour of a child's birth, and that he may tear it
from the breast of its mother, in the act of afford-
ing it the nourishment which supports its life.

This is a very strong case. Here is an English-
woman possessed of property, married to a needy
French emigrant, whose only complaint against
his wife appears to have been her reluctance to
will away that property in his favour. The circumstances under which the child was taken were
most gross, and such as would seem the act of a
savage rather than of one educated in a civilized
country. The child itself was only a few months
old ; unweaned, and utterly dependant on the mother; but because, as Lord Ellenborough observed,
" there was no pretence it had been *injured* by
want of nurture," that is, because the father, after

cruelly taking it from the breast of its mother, supplied it with another nurse, he was held not to have abused his "right," but to have the same claim to the custody of his child as any other man.

---

*SKINNER *v.* SKINNER, A.D. 1824. *In the Court of Common Pleas.*

This case is chiefly remarkable, inasmuch as the *effect* of the decision given, was to leave the infant not even in the custody of the father, but *in the custody of the woman with whom the father was living in adultery.*

It appeared that the husband had treated his wife with the utmost cruelty and brutality, and that, in consequence of such treatment, a separation took place : that he afterwards lived and cohabited with a woman named Anne Deverall, and that, at first, the child (who was *under six years of age* at the time of these proceedings) was permitted to reside with its mother ; but subsequently Mr. Skinner caused a writ of *habeas corpus* to be issued out of the Court of King's Bench, and on the parties attending at the chambers of Chief (then Mr.) Justice Best, it was agreed that the child should be placed under the care of a third person.

---

* 9 Moore, 278.

Becoming afterwards discontented with this arrangement, the father took the infant away from the third party, by stratagem and fraud, and being subsequently confined for debt in Horsemonger-lane goal, he left it in the care and custody of his mistress, Anne Deverall, who brought it to see him every day, and continued to cohabit with him when in prison.

Application was then made for a writ of *habeas corpus*, directing William Skinner and Anne Deverall to bring up the infant, that it might be delivered over *to the care of the mother*. Affidavits were made, setting forth the ill-treatment she had sustained, the fact of the husband's adultery, removal of the child from the charge of the person with whom he had agreed that it should remain, &c.

It is remarkable that, in arguing on behalf of the mother in this case, Mr. Sergeant Lawes cited no less than FOUR *instances in which the Court had interfered to protect the mothers of* BASTARD *children.* The case of *ex parte Knee*,* where the Court held that the mother of an infant illegitimate child was entitled to the custody of it, *in preference to the father, although, from his circumstances, he might be better able to educate it.* The King *v.* Hopkins,† in which the Court granted a writ of *habeas corpus*, to bring up the

* 1 New Rep. 148.   † 7 East, 579.

body of a bastard child, within the age of nurture, for the purpose of *restoring it to the custody of the mother, from whose quiet possession it was taken, at one time by fraud, and afterwards by force.* THE KING *v.* SOPER,* where, in like manner, the putative father obtained possession of his bastard child by fraud, and the Court ordered it *to be returned to the mother;* and THE KING *v.* MOSELY,† in which the same point was decided. The case of BLISSET‡ was also mentioned, as proving that where the father appeared to be an improper person to have the care of the child, and it was of too tender an age to choose for itself, the Court of King's Bench had a discretionary power to assign the custody of the infant to a third person, on the ground that the power of the parent is subordinate to the authority of the State, in the education of a child, as in other respects. And these points were further pressed upon the attention of the Court—namely, that the husband was confined within the walls of a prison; was, even there, living in a state of adultery; and had broken the agreement made, that the child should remain with a third person, and removed it by stratagem and fraud.

In spite, however, of these arguments, the decision was given *against the mother's claim,* on the ground that the Court of King's Bench had " *no*

---

* 5. Term Rep. 278.   † 5. East, 224. n.   ‡ Lofft, 748.

POWER *to interfere ;*" and Lord Chief Justice Best expressed himself in the following terms :— " When this case first came before me at Chambers, I felt considerable difficulty, and thought that, under the circumstances, neither father nor mother was entitled to have the custody of the child; and it was there agreed on by both parents that it should be placed under the care of a third person. Still the father had a power *to take it away* ; and although the Court might direct the child to be brought up by a writ of *habeas corpus*, yet the difficulty is, *what is to be done with it now it is before us ?* I was referred to Blissett's case, and it certainly is extremely strong to shew that the power of assigning the custody of a child brought before the Court of King's Bench was discretionary, if the father *appeared to be an improper person to take it.* I therefore thought that the most prudent course would be to assign it to the care of a third person, and which was acceded to by *both* its parents. But it now appears that the father has removed the child, and has the custody of it himself, and no authority has been cited to shew that this Court has jurisdiction *to take it out of such custody*, FOR THE PURPOSE OF DELIVERING IT TO THE MOTHER."

In the course of these observations, his Lordship referred to the Court of Chancery, as having a power *superior* to that of the King's Bench, as representing the King as *Parens Patriæ ;* and he affirmed that that *other* Court *might* accordingly, under certain circumstances, control the right of a father to the possession of his child, and appoint a proper person to watch over its morals, and see that it receive proper education and instruction. Undoubtedly, the Court of Chancery HAS such a power; but the question is, under what circumstances it will EXERT any authority. It does not appear that Mrs. Skinner presented any petition to that Court; but in the cases of Mrs. Ball and Mrs. Greenhill, (which are given at page 22 and 28) it will be seen, that although in *both* instances the husband was living in adultery, and the wife was a person in all respects fit to keep and educate her children, the Court did not consider itself *authorized to control the custody of the father.* A woman, circumstanced as Mrs. Skinner was, goes to the Court of King's Bench and the Court says, " your case is a hard one, but *we* have NO POWER *to interfere.*" She goes to the Court of Chancery, and there the answer is—" We certainly *have* a power to control the father's right, under circumstances of gross misconduct, ill usage of his children, or waste of their property; but we cannot consider the fact of your husband forsaking *you*, and living openly with a mistress, as *gross misconduct*, nor as any proof that he will neglect his children's interests, or waste their property; *therefore* WE cannot interfere, any more than the Court of

King's Bench. The law is, that the father has a RIGHT to take the children from you, and to bar your access to them if he chooses, and we have *no power* to compel him to act otherwise."

Mrs. Skinner's case is, perhaps, as strong a proof as could be given, that the power to restore legitimate children to the care of the mother, *should* exist in one or both of these Courts; since, as I have already said, the effect of the decision here was to leave the child in the same custody as before; and that custody was *not* the custody of the father, (however it might be nominally held to be such,) but the custody of THE WOMAN WITH WHOM HE WAS LIVING. Now, there is much talk of protecting the *child* from ill-usage, but is there no way of protecting the *mother?* Can any thing be conceived more bitter than the situation of this woman, compelled to resign her child,—her own flesh and blood,—into the hands of one whom she must naturally regard with distrust, hatred, and loathing, as the person who had seduced from her the affections of her husband, and who had been, probably, the cause of all she had endured? Is it natural that she should expect such a one to shew kindness to her infant? or, if shewn, is there not something revolting in the idea of this unconscious child lavishing its tenderness on the woman who had so bitterly wronged its mother? Is it just to take it from that wife and mother, anxious as she must be for the welfare and purity

of mind of her little one, and pollute its innocence by giving it up to the strange woman and
adulteress ?   And can it be believed that a decision would be made in an English court of justice,
calculated to produce such a result?   I do not
say that the Court decided that this woman should
have the child, but that such was the *effect* of the
decision which, under the present state of the
law, they felt themselves *legally bound* to make.
It is not of the POWER OF THE COURT TO MAKE
THAT DECISION that I complain ; but, on the
contrary, of THE WANT OF POWER TO MAKE ANY
OTHER.   It is against all our ideas of natural justice that the mistress of this adulterous husband
should forcibly retain the legitimate offspring of
his deserted wife, and the law *must* be defective
which permits such an abuse of natural rights.

It is constantly urged that a measure of which
the principles are correct, and which *in general*
may be said to act well, is not to be considered
faulty because it either cannot be made to
apply to isolated instances of wrong, or acts upon
them with an apparent increase of *oppressive*
instead of *remedial* power : and such I admit to
be the case : a mill-wheel may be excellently
contrived which yet does not grind every separate grain that passes under it : but I deny that
the principle of *this* law, *does* work well—(if indeed that can be called *a law* which is rather
the absence of one—the non-existence of a power

of protection for the woman.) I assert that in every instance which I shall give, it has worked *ill;* and those instances have been chosen, not as isolated examples of injustice and oppression, but as the instances readiest to be come at, and the best known, because preserved among the legal reports, and quoted as precedents.

The above case of Skinner is constantly quoted as a precedent ; it therefore cannot be said that it is an isolated instance of the bad effects of the law, for the decision given on that occasion is made to support *other* decisions in similar cases, and should an instance recur, point for point the same, and the most eloquent counsel at the bar were to urge the hardship of abandoning the child to the mistress of the husband, the reply of the Court would be, that *it had been held in the case of Skinner v. Skinner, that they had* "NO POWER" *to interfere.*

This case, therefore, must be taken with the rest, and being so taken, is a strong argument against the existence of the father's absolute and uncontrolled right to dispose of his infant children.

C

Case of Mrs. M'Clellan,* a.d. 1830.
Court of King's Bench.

This case, like the foregoing, is one well known
and constantly quoted as a precedent, and one
which cannot fail to excite compassion for the
mother, since the child of whom she desired to
retain possession, was afflicted with a disease by
which she had lost her other children, and this
state of its health was the only reason urged
against the exertion of ' *The father's Right.*'

It does not appear in the brief report from
which the facts of this case are taken, what was
the cause of the separation between the father
and mother; but *being* so separated, the father
had taken this little girl, a child of tender years,
and placed her at school, where she had remained
for some time. Becoming afterwards diseased
with scrofula, and requiring constant care and
attention, the mother persuaded the governess
to allow her to take it away, promising to restore
it in a short time. The child continued ill, and
was not brought back; and the father procured
a writ of habeas corpus to bring up the infant
from the custody of the mother and restore it to
that of the schoolmistress.

* Dowling's Practical Cases, Vol. i. p. 81.

It was argued for the mother, that the child was in a very delicate state of health, *that two of her children had died of this very complaint, and that the mother only struggled to retain possession of it, that she might personally bestow on it all the tenderness and attention its state required;* which she had done ever since it was delivered up to her by the governess; and a hope was expressed that under the peculiar circumstances, the child would not be delivered over to the father by the judgment of the Court.

Mr. Justice Patteson, however, decided *against the mother's claim;* quoting de Manneville as a precedent that the law was perfectly clear as to the right of the father to the possession of his legitimate children, *of whatever age they be;* and also referring to the case of *Skinner,* as one in which the Court had doubted its authority to interfere, (and where as we have already seen the Court did *not* interfere). His Lordship in conclusion remarked, " There is nothing suggested which leads one to suppose that any *illusage* has been exercised by the father, or by the schoolmistress with whom he wishes his child to be placed. I feel myself, therefore, bound to say that the child must be delivered up to Miss——, whom the father has named. *It might be better, as the child is in a delicate state of health, that it* SHOULD *be with the mother;* but WE cannot make any order on that point."

The matter was thus brought to a conclusion. As I have already stated it to be my intention, after the instances selected for the purpose have been given, to make some general observations on the effects of the law, I will not further remark on the present example, than to point out the obvious fact, that no one of the causes which might be supposed to justify the father's cruelty, appear in the report. No misconduct was alleged on the part of the mother, and so far from its being for the child's interest or comfort that it should be so removed, it was expressly stated that the governess was persuaded to allow the mother to take it away, *in order that it might receive, in its sick and diseased condition, a care more vigilant and affectionate than it could otherwise obtain.*   Mr. Justice Patteson remarked, "it is not pretended that the child has been ill-treated ;" so gross a cruelty as the *intentional* ill-usage of a helpless child, confided even to hired attendants, is, to the honour of human nature, extremely rare: but there is a wide difference between the absence of all intentional cruelty, and the devoted watchfulness and care of a mother, especially in a case like this, where, from the circumstance of her former children having suffered from the same complaint, the mother may be supposed to have earned the experience of what was best to be done. It is impossible from these brief legal reports, where nothing is set down more than is absolutely neces-

sary to explain the decision given, to collect all
the circumstances which might tend either to
aggravate or excuse the apparent harshness displayed towards a woman in Mrs. M'Clellan's
anxious and painful position; but enough has
been shown to entitle this case to rank among
those in which " The father's Right" has been un-
duly exercised ; and certainly to prove that NO *circumstance of hardship, as regards* THE MOTHER'S
FEELINGS, *weighs with the decision of the Courts,*
although they are so repeatedly said to exert " a
discretionary power."   Mr. Justice Patteson did
indeed give it as his private opinion that the sickly
child would be best in the custody of its own mother,
but, as a judge, he considered he was bound to
decide *against* that mother, or rather that he
had "NO POWER *to interfere.*"   The same remark
made in the foregoing example (Skinner *v.*
Skinner) will apply here; namely, that the power
to interfere OUGHT to exist somewhere, and that
that power should be exerted to protect the mother's claim to children under the age of nurture ;
indeed it may be questioned whether the law,
arbitrary as it is, is not *strained*, when the father's
custody is interpreted to be, the *custody of any
stranger the father may choose to appoint.*   There
is something revolting in the idea of this little
sickly wretch being forcibly taken from its mother,
and returned to its schoolmistress, merely because
it was the father's will and pleasure that the me-

lancholy satisfaction of nursing it should be denied to his wife; more especially when it is remembered that she had already laid two in the grave, and that no reason was assigned for taking it from her.

BALL *v.* BALL,* A. D. 1827.—*Court of Chancery.*

This case differs from the three which have already been given, in as much as the child was *above the age of nurture,* and the mother petitioned EITHER to be permitted the custody of her daughter (she offering to maintain her at her own expence), or, failing in that, *to be permitted access to her* at all convenient times. This petition was to *the Court of Chancery ;* and it will be seen that the superior authority to control the father's right, to which allusion was made in the cases of Skinner and M'Clellan, was not exerted in her favour. The report before me being sufficiently familiar, and devoid of legal technicality of expression, I shall give it nearly *verbatim.*

Mr. Shadwell (the present Vice-Chancellor) and Mr. Bickersteth, (the present Master of the Rolls) for the petitioners (Mrs. Ball, and Emily Owen Ball, her daughter), stated that the father was living in habitual adultery with another woman,

---

* Simon's **Reports**, vol. ii. page 35.

on account of which Mrs. Ball had obtained a divorce in the Ecclesiastical Courts.

The Vice-Chancellor observed:—

" *The Court has nothing to do with the fact of the father's adultery, unless the father brings the child into contact with the woman.* All the cases on this subject go upon that distinction, where adultery is the ground of a petition for depriving the father of his Common Law Right over the custody of his children."

(It was explained that the mother's object was not to deprive the father of this right, and that her petition was in the alternative, and merely prayed that *if the daughter was not allowed to live with her, she might at least have liberty of access.* The argument was then continued). " The child formerly lived with her mother, and occasionally went to visit her father. On one of these occasions, the father (without any communication with the mother) detained the daughter, and sent her to a school. *The mother was for a long time ignorant what had become of her child;* and when, after most persevering search, she found out the school at which she had been placed, the mistress refused to allow the mother to see the child except in her presence. We admit there is no cause for taking away the father's authority, but submit that *there is very good cause for granting the* OTHER ALTERNATIVE *of the prayer of the petition,*" (namely, free access to the child).

" The daughter, when with her father, is living in a house where there is no society except that of a female servant of all work; but when she is with her mother, she has the attention of a mother whose conduct is entirely unexceptionable, and who has always endeavoured to impress upon her child a proper regard towards the father; and in one letter from Mr. Ball he thus expresses himself: ' *I should be most happy to see my child put under her mother's protection.*' In another, ' *The charge of my seeking to deprive the mother of her child is most false; if it had been true, my character would be stamped as that of a villain.*' Yet subsequently to these letters he secretes the child from her mother, and sends her away."

" The affidavits go on to state that the father's conduct was so gross and violent towards Mrs. Ball, when she went to him to make inquiries as to the daughter's residence, that it was dangerous for her to be in his presence. THE QUESTION REALLY IS, WHETHER A CHILD IS TO BE DEPRIVED BY THE BRUTAL CONDUCT OF THE FATHER, OF THE COMPANY, ADVICE, AND PROTECTION OF A MOTHER, AGAINST WHOM NO IMPUTATION CAN BE RAISED ?"

The Vice-Chancellor said:

" Some conduct, on the part of the father, *with reference to the management and education of the child must be shown, to warrant an interference with his* LEGAL RIGHT ; and I am bound to say, that in this case there does not appear to me to be sufficient to deprive the father of his Common Law Right to the care and custody of his child. It resolves itself into a case for authorities; and I must consider *what has been looked upon as the law on this point.* I do not know that I have ANY AUTHORITY TO INTERFERE. I do not know of any case similar to this, which would authorize my making the order sought, in *either* alternative. *If any could be found, I would most gladly adopt it; for, in a* MORAL *point of view, I know of* NO ACT MORE HARSH OR CRUEL, *than depriving a mother of proper intercourse with her child.*

"I was myself counsel in two cases, in which Lord Eldon refused petitions precisely similar. Smith *v.* Smith (one of them), was *precisely* similar in its facts to the present case, except that the father's object *there was to compel the mother, by such means as are now complained of, to give up to him some property, which was settled to her own separate use.* My course of argument in that case was, *that as the law allowed* THE MOTHERS OF BASTARDS *to retain possession of their children till the age of seven, a fortiori, must the law allow* THE CARE OF LEGITIMATE CHILDREN TO BE VESTED IN THE MOTHER (the child in that case was under seven). The Lord Chancellor, however, refused the order, and before any further proceedings were had, *either the mother's or the child's death determined the question.* That was a very strong

case ; *yet the Lord Chancellor held that the Court
had no jurisdiction.*

After some further observations, the petition
in behalf of Mrs. Ball and her daughter was dismissed ; this Court of superior authority deciding, that it had no more power than the Court
of King's Bench to restore a LEGITIMATE child
to the mother from whom it had been taken by
force and fraud, *even where the husband was
living in open adultery;* and not only the Court
had not power to *restore* the infant, but it was
not able even to order that the mother might
from time to time *see* the child so taken from
her !

I quite agree with Mr. Ball's own view of the
subject, that *such conduct would stamp a man's character as that of a villain;* and one great argument
against the existence of this absolute right on the
part of the father is, that it can scarcely exist
except for the purpose of abuse ; for it will be
difficult to find a single instance of a JUST, HO-
NOURABLE, and HUMANE man, desirous of taking
infant children from a mother *not guilty of sin,*
although that mother should be unfortunately
separated from him on other accounts.   On the
contrary, examples might be given where such
men have ' leaned to mercy's side,' even when
sternness would have appeared justifiable.   The
power, therefore, given by the law, rests with
men who, like De Manneville and Smith, use it

*as an instrument of torture, to force an unwilling
gift of property;* or those who, like Mr. Ball
and others, whose cases are here given, appear
*to exert it from wanton cruelty, or from motives of
vengeance and hatred to the woman.*

In this, as in the previous example, there is no
pretence that the mother was unfit to have the
custody, or that it was in any way for the child's
interest that it should be separated from her.
Mrs. Ball's reputation was free from all shadow
of reproach ; she was a fond and attentive parent, and she was able to maintain and educate
her daughter, without any pecuniary assistance
whatever from the father.   Every possible argument that could be urged, was *in favour* of her
retaining possession of the child ; and we have,
besides, the expression of the Vice-Chancellor's
feelings and opinions on the subject, AT DIRECT
VARIANCE WITH HIS LEGAL DECISION.   It is fair,
then, to number this among the instances which
prove the necessity for a revision of *that law, of
which the judge himself appeared to doubt the justice, and to admit the inhumanity.*   It is fair to expect, that the day will come, when some better
answer may be made in a Court, assuming authority to protect the subject, than that here
given, namely, *"We have* NO POWER *to interfere."*
If ever circumstances warranted interference,
those under which Mrs. Ball was deprived of her
young daughter, would seem to require it.   The
husband had been legally separated from her on

account of *his* conduct ; he was of so violent and
furious a disposition, that it was *dangerous* for
this unhappy woman to approach his presence,
merely to ask the residence of her child; he had
obtained possession by fraud, and sent it away
without even permitting the mother to know of
its removal.   In short, there is no possible way
in which we can reconcile the decision given
with our ideas of justice.   The decision was *es-
sentially* UNJUST, and is, besides, mischievous in
its effect, since it establishes a precedent for a
like ill-usage of some other sufferer, and a cer-
tainty of impunity on the part of the sinner ;
both which mischief and injustice might be pre-
vented by the acknowledgment.of THE NATURAL
CLAIM OF THE MOTHER, where nothing has occurred by which she can be said to have forfeited
that claim.

---

*MRS. GREENHILL'S CASE, 1835.

The case I am now about to enter into, affords
the strongest argument that can be given
against the absolute right of the father over
the persons of his infant children ; since more
cruel, unjust, unmanly dealing, or more gross
and open defiance of all decency and social

---

* Court of Chancery and Court of King's Bench.

right, never was displayed than in the reported conduct of the husband. If I were to make my stand on a single case, I would make it on THIS, and say that the law which permitted such a decision in such a case, is INHUMAN, IMMORAL, AND FOUNDED ON NO CONCEIVABLE PRINCIPLE OF NATURAL JUSTICE.

In the year 1829 Miss Macdonald, daughter of Col. Macdonald of Exeter, was married to B. C. Greenhill, Esq. They had three children; Lavinia, Flora-Macdonald, and Clari; *all severally under six years of age at the time of the separation;* the youngest being but two years and a half old.

In Sept. 1835, Mrs. Greenhill (being then at Weymouth for the benefit of her health, with her three little girls, and Mr. Greenhill absent in his pleasure yacht) received intelligence that her husband was unfaithful to her, and had for more than a year been intimate with a female of the name of Graham, with whom he had cohabited both in London and at Portsmouth, passing her off as his wife, and even allowing her to assume his name. Distracted with sorrow and indignation, Mrs. Greenhill set out for Exeter where her mother resided, in order to obtain the support and advice of her family under these trying circumstances. Her brother Capt. R. Macdonald, and her sister, accompanied her back to Winterborne (one stage short of Weymouth), where the two ladies remained till Capt.

Macdonald having proceeded alone to Weymouth,
and broken up the establishment there, brought
the children to their mother; the party then returned to Exeter, and Mrs. Greenhill remained
under the protection of her own family, and
instituted proceedings in the proper Courts, for
separation from her husband (on the ground of
adultery) and for alimony.

On Mr. Greenhill being informed of the discovery that had been made, and the plans his
wife had in consequence adopted, he became
anxious to prevent the proceedings in the Ecclesiastical Courts, and accordingly sent his attorney
Mr. B. to Exeter to obtain an interview with
Mrs. Greenhill, and induce her if possible to relinquish the proceedings. The outraged wife however expressed her resolution to adhere to the
measures adopted in unison with the opinions of
her own family, and on Mr. B. informing her
that Mr. Greenhill was willing to give her such
a provision as it was likely the Court would
award her for alimony, she replied that she would
accept "nothing but what *the law* would give
her."

Finding that Mrs. Greenhill would not consent
to forego the suit, her husband changed his tone,
and Mr. B. was instructed to *write to her*, and
make her aware of the insult and injury which
would be *added* to the wrong she had already suffered, in the event of her persisting to go into

the Ecclesiastical Court; which was accordingly done.

Mrs. Greenhill had, on arriving at Exeter, sent her maid to Knowle (the former residence of herself and husband), with orders to pack up her wardrobe and jewels, as also the children's clothes, and bring them to Mrs. Macdonald's house; Mrs. Greenhill having resolved never again to return to Knowle Hall. This was not overlooked in the letter alluded to, (though, in an affidavit subsequently made by Mr. Greenhill, he expressly swears, that the jewels were bought with part of the portion paid him with his wife, by her father, Colonel Macdonald.)

Mr. B. begins by expressing his regret, that he has not been able to effect an amicable arrangement between Mr. G. and her husband; in conclusion, he *begs most distinctly to state,* " *that unless the* LEGAL RIGHT TO RETAIN THE CHILDREN CAN BE SUCCESSFULLY SUPPORTED BY HER ADVISERS, SHE WILL NOT HAVE THAT PERMISSION ACCORDED TO HER; *and the jewels having been taken from Knowle Hall, without either the knowledge or consent of Mr. G., the party who committed the offence* WILL BE SEVERELY PUNISHED FOR HER RASHNESS (!) *unless the jewels, and other valuables, are forthwith returned; as Mrs. G. must be well aware that she has no* LEGAL *right whatever to them; and as she only requires, and will only have, what the law may award her in one sense, so, on the other hand, she cannot expect more yielded to her, all reconciliation having been rejected by herself.*

" *Mr. B. makes, therefore, on Mr. Greenhill's behalf, three distinct demands :—*

" 1. *The return of all Mr. Greenhill's jewels, taken from Knowle.*

" 2. *An order, that the* CARRIAGE *should be delivered up to Mr. Browne* THIS EVENING.

" 3. *And, the most important of all, that the* CHILDREN SHALL BE PLACED UNDER MR. B.'s PROTECTION, *to be taken to Knowle.*"

We make no comment on this letter; Mr. B. was only performing a duty in doing the best for his client, according to his judgment and ability ; but what shall be said of the husband, who thus persisted in insulting and harassing a young and unoffending wife, one who had been an invalid for some time, and whose health was further injured by the very unexpected sorrows which awaited her?

Mrs. Greenhill did not obey the command of this letter, and the next step taken by her husband was to move for a writ of *habeas corpus,* commanding her to produce the three children on the 28th October, at the house of Justice Patteson. As soon as the writ was issued, and before its return, the mother instituted a suit in Chancery, for the purpose of making the children wards of that Court ; and a petition was presented praying the PROTECTION OF THE COURT, and that a proper guardian might be appointed. Mrs. Greenhill's principal fear seems to have been, that if her children (who were accustomed to the tenderest care, and were very delicate) were taken from her, they would be delivered over to the care of her mother-in-law, Mrs. Mary Tyler Greenhill, a person represented as of a very violent temper, and particularly unfit to have the care of them, having always disliked her daughter-in-law, and having shewn so marked a neglect of these her little grandchildren, as to write a letter or letters *forbidding them to be sent to visit her ;* and on one occasion, meeting them by accident, while walking with their nurse, she spoke to a child who was on a visit to Mrs. Greenhill's little girls, *but took no notice whatever of her own grandchildren.* (This lady, in a subsequent affidavit, partially admitted these facts, and accounted for them by insisting, that since her son had married, he did not devote his time or attention to his mother as before, and she therefore considered Mrs. Greenhill had *weaned his heart from her !*)

On the night of the 28th October, in obedience to the writ of *habeas corpus*, Mrs. Greenhill having arrived with her children from Exeter, appeared with them at Mr. Justice Patteson's. Some argument by counsel on each side took place before his Lordship, who ultimately allowed

the matter to stand over till the evening of
Thursday, the 5th November, the children meanwhile remaining with the mother, and their presence being dispensed with by the consent of all
parties.

On the morning of Thursday, the 5th of November, the petition in Chancery was heard by
the Vice-Chancellor, and six affidavits were read
before him, the substance of which was as follows :—

That Mr. Greenhill had, as already stated,
carried on an adulterous connection with Mrs.
Graham, for more than a twelvemonth ; and
that *he positively refused to part with her* (although
he affirmed, that he had expressed his regret and
contrition to his wife, and made overtures of reconciliation); that on being told by his wife that
she had heard he had taken a house for three
years for this woman, he replied, " it was no bu-
siness of *hers* if he had taken it for *ten* years ;"
that he allowed Mrs. Graham to take his wife's
name, and call herself " Mrs. Greenhill ;" and at
other times *he* called himself " Mr. Graham ;"
and that he desired the servant, who also occasionally waited on his wife, to wait on this woman,
and drive her out in his cab; that he left his
wife at Weymouth, to go and live with Mrs.
Graham at Portsmouth ; and that he took her
with him in his yacht, &c. ; in short, that as to
the act of adultery, it was neither attempted to

be concealed or denied ; but, on the contrary, he had admitted it to his wife's uncle and other relatives, and expressed his determination to persist in the intimacy he had formed.

That Mrs. Greenhill firmly believed, that her children, if taken from her, would be *prevented from seeing her*, and delivered over to Mrs. Mary Tyler Greenhill as aforesaid ; that the said Mrs. Mary Tyler Greenhill had not only abused and quarrelled with her daughter-in-law, and refused to see her grandchildren, but that she had been at law for years *with her own son ;* and that so bitter was their estrangement, that Mr. Greenhill had said to a friend who advised him to be reconciled to his mother, that such reconciliation was *impossible ;* and that they were in fact *only drawn together by the anger of Mr. Greenhill against his wife, and since the quarrel between the parties.* That for these and other reasons, neither Mrs. M. Tyler Greenhill, nor Mr. Greenhill himself, were fit persons to have the custody of these infant children, and that their mother *was* a fit and proper person, and *neither her husband, nor any other person, alleged anything to the contrary, nor had there been at any time a shadow of imputation against her.* That Mrs. Greenhill's own mother, Mrs. Macdonald (who had always been on good terms with her son-in-law, and had shewn him great affection, especially in nursing him through the cholera, when every one else,

from fear or prudence, withdrew from the house),
*was willing to receive his wife and children; to
give them a permanent home with her; and was
also willing, that the father should come and visit
his children, at her house, as often as he pleased.*
That Mrs. G. was fondly and devotedly attached
to her little girls, and had never been separated
from them; and that the father had always been
in the habit of leaving them under her sole custody and control during his absence from home;
and though it was affirmed, on the one hand,
that Mr. Greenhill was a fond and attentive
father, yet it was sworn in contradiction, that one
of the little children being brought into the room
with several strangers, asked Mrs. Greenhill's
uncle, " if *he* was papa," from which it was argued, that they had not been in the frequent
habit of seeing him, since his connection with
Mrs. Graham. Finally, it was sworn, that Mrs.
Greenhill had always fulfilled, to the utmost, her
duties as a wife and mother; and that there was
no possible ground for depriving her of her three
little girls, but, on the contrary, every reason
why she should be permitted the care of them;
and that her health, already very delicate, had
suffered so much from the terror, agony, and
sorrow, which she had lately endured, that it was
expected she would sink under the blow (if inflicted) of that forcible separation.

All this having been sworn, the Vice-Chancellor gave his decision, namely, " *That however bad and immoral Mr. Greenhill's conduct might be, unless that conduct was brought so under the notice of the children as to render it probable that their minds would be contaminated, the Court of Chancery had* NO AUTHORITY TO INTERFERE *with the common law right of the father, and that he had not* THE POWER *to order that Mrs. Greenhill should even* SEE *her children as a matter of right.*" He accordingly dismissed the petition, the mother's separate claim not being acknowledged by the Court. Similar affidavits were read again the same evening, before Mr. Justice Patteson, who was attended by counsel on each side. His Lordship took time to consider these affidavits, and said that before he decided, he would consult the other judges.

On the 10th November, his decision was given *against* the mother's claim, and he signed an order that Mrs. Greenhill should forthwith deliver up to Mr. Greenhill his three infant children.

On the 12th, that order was made a rule of Court, and *served personally* by Mr. Greenhill on his wife, of whom he, at the same time, demanded the children. Mrs. Greenhill gave only a written reply, couched as follows :—

" *Mrs. Greenhill is desirous of paying the utmost respect to the Court; but as she feels that the health and comfort of her three infants (under the*

*age of six years), will be destroyed by their removal
from her care, she prefers sacrificing* HERSELF, *if it
be called for, rather than so sacrifice her* CHILDREN;
*being well assured, that their removal is with the
ultimate intention of excluding her from all communication with them."*

Mr. Greenhill's next step was to make affidavit of the service of the rule, and of his wife's
refusal to part with her infants, in order to obtain
a writ of attachment against her; i. e. *to cause
her to be imprisoned* for contempt of Court.

Mrs. Greenhill, on her part, obtained a rule
nisi in the Court of King's Bench, calling on her
husband to shew cause why Mr. Justice Patteson's order should not be set aside, and the children remain with their mother.

A short delay was granted to Mrs. Greenhill
to shew cause why an attachment should not issue
against her; and the same delay was allowed to
Mr. Greenhill to shew cause why Mr. Justice
Patteson's order should not be discharged.

The matter was argued on the 24th November
—Mr. Sergeant Talfourd appearing for Mr.
Greenhill.   At the conclusion of the learned
Sergeant's address, Lord Denman observed that
it would be better that some arrangement should
take place, so that *both* parties should have access
to the children, and to effect that object a further
delay was given.   On the following day, Mr.
Sergeant Wilde, Mr. Sergeant Talfourd, Mr.

Greenhill and his attorney, and Mrs. Mary Tyler Greenhill, met for the purpose suggested by Lord Denman, but owing, as affirmed, to the obstinacy and perverseness of this lady (who seemed determined to prevent her son from coming to any reasonable terms), no arrangement was entered into.

On the 30th instant Mr. Greenhill declared, through his attorney, that no further steps would be taken for such arrangement ; and demanded to see the children.   Mrs. Greenhill becoming alarmed lest they should be seized from her, withdrew precipitately and left the kingdom, taking with her her three little girls.

In January the matter was again argued (Mrs. Greenhill being still abroad), and the rule obtained by her, to set aside Justice Patteson's order, was discharged; or in other words, the last attempt made by this unhappy and unoffending woman LEGALLY *to retain possession of her infant children* FAILED ; *the decision of the judges being given* AGAINST THE MOTHER'S CLAIM.

In the course of the arguments advanced by the counsel on either side, at the different periods of this cause, the following observations were made in support of Mrs. Greenhill's case.

" The children are all females, and infants of tender years, and whom it appears most UNNATURAL to tear from a mother who is devotedly attached to them, against whom not a shadow of

imputation rests, and whom her husband does not
hesitate to admit is in every respect a fit and
proper person to have the care and custody of
them. ILLEGITIMATE *children under the age of
nurture* (which has been held to be seven years),
*cannot by law be taken from the mother, and it
seems most* UNNATURAL *and* UNJUST *that* LEGITI-
MATE *children should be in a worse position. It
cannot be denied that it has been held to be law that
an infant may, by the father, be torn from the
breast, but it is submitted* THAT THERE IS GROUND
FOR A REVISION OF THAT DECISION."

    " Mrs. G. does not dispute her husband's right
to the custody of the children. She has offered
to take them to any part of England Mr. G. shall
prescribe, and to obey his injunctions, *provided
she be not wholly separated from them.* The
question in this case is, *not whether the rights of
the father are paramount,* BUT WHETHER THE LAW
IS ENTIRELY REGARDLESS OF THE NATURAL CLAIM
OF THE MOTHER."

    " The mother does not even insist that the
children shall be in the same house with her, *but
only that she shall have access to her children.* The
real question is, WHETHER THE RIGHT OF THE
FATHER AMOUNTS TO THE EXCLUSION OF THE
MOTHER."—" Where the father applies, as in the
present case, not for the purpose of really assert-
ing his own right, but MERELY FOR THE PURPOSE
OF EXCLUDING THE MOTHER FROM HAVING ACCESS

TO HER CHILDREN, this Court will (in the exercise of its discretion) *refuse to permit so harsh and cruel a proceeding.*"

" It is not contended that this Court has power to take the child from the father, but surely the Court will pause before it makes an order to deprive children of so tender an age of the care and superintendence of the mother. *The Court may be quiescent, and is not bound to act.* If this rule is made absolute, Mrs. Greenhill will have no means of superintending the education of her infant daughters, nor will she be able even to see them, for in Ball *v.* Ball the Vice-Chancellor decided *that he had no power to order the father to permit the mother to have access to her child.*"

" Here, the fault and blame of the parents not living together, must be imputed to the father."

In opposition to these remarks, and in support of the " Father's Right," as exercised by Mr. Greenhill, it was observed :—

" There is no doubt that BY LAW the father is entitled to the custody of his children. The wife is *not* entitled to such custody in opposition to the claims of the husband."

" There is no ground for setting aside the order of Mr. Justice Patteson. *One alleged reason is, that the children are within the age of nurture.* That is not a sufficient reason. THE LAW has given the custody of the children, in cases of unhappy disputes between the husband and wife, to the husband. Of *illegitimate* children, it is true that they cannot be separated from the mother during the period of nurture, but THE LAW *recognises no such principle with respect to legitimate children.*"

" In Rex *v.* De Manneville, (a much stronger case, since the infant was only eight months old) this question was much considered, *and that* CASE IS AN EXPRESS AUTHORITY *to shew that Mrs. Greenhill has no right to detain these children.* The case of DE MANNEVILLE is recognised and commented on in the case of McCLELLAN. In ex parte SKINNER, all the cases are collected, and the true distinction is taken,—that *this Court has* NO *discretionary power* to control the right of a father to the possession of his child."

" *The second ground for setting aside Justice Patteson's order, is the immorality of the father.* It is laid down by Lord Eldon that this is a matter within the jurisdiction of the Chancellor only ; but *assuming that this Court has the same jurisdiction as the Lord Chancellor,—will this Court* DIFFER *from the Vice Chancellor, who upon the statement of the circumstances now presented to this Court,* REFUSED TO INTERFERE WITH THE RIGHT OF THE FATHER ? In BALL *v.* BALL, the Vice Chancellor is reported to have said, " the Court has nothing to do with the fact of the father's adultery, unless he bring the child into contact with the woman. *In ex parte Skinner, not only was the husband living in adultery, but he actually had entrusted the child to the woman with whom he was living in adultery,* AND YET THE COURT ALLOWED HIM TO RETAIN THE CHILD."

Lord Denman, in giving his decision, said— " This is a rule obtained for setting aside an order, which directs that the children of Mr. Greenhill should be delivered up to him; and as, unfortunately, the attempts to arrange the matter have failed, we are now bound to pronounce what we believe to be THE LAW upon the subject. There is no doubt whatever, that where a father has the custody of his children, he is not to be deprived of them, except under such circumstances of misconduct as do not occur in the present case ; for though Mr. Greenhill is charged with misconduct, yet there is nothing in the case stated, with respect to his conduct, which has ever been held *sufficient to deprive* A FATHER *of the custody of his children."*

" It is true the father has formed an illicit connection ; but it is not pretended that the woman with whom the connection has been formed was living in the father's house, *or that his conduct in this connection has been marked with any offensive indecency.* As far as the husband's assurances may be taken, they are distinctly given, that he would not bring the children into contact with the woman in question ; and it is not to be presumed that he would violate the assurances he has thus given." And finally his Lordship observed :—

" We do not feel that we could make any
modified order ; and we cannot entertain any
doubt that my brother Patteson acted rightly."

Now, without discussing whether the circumstances of Mr. Greenhill permitting his mistress
to bear his wife's name ; to be waited on by his
wife's servant ; to sail in the yacht in which he
had just before taken his wife ; or the fact of his
admitting to his wife's relations that this woman
was his mistress ; refusing to part with her, and
admitting that he lived with her as Mr. Graham ;
were or were not circumstances which *marked
his conduct in the connection with offensive indecency ;* and allowing the negative proof afforded
by the long concealment of that connection, that
some decency *was* observed with respect to its
management, yet we may be permitted to ask
whether it would not be an improvement in the
law if the question were not so much " *Why
should this man, in spite of his adultery,* NOT *take
away his children ?*" as " *Why should this woman
who has in no way offended, be* DEPRIVED *of her
children ?*" especially as there is no question but
the father would in *all* cases have whatever access
he pleased to his offspring.

Suppose the case to be reversed ; suppose *a
woman* to have carried on an intrigue for a year,
and to have conducted it with so much *decency,*
i. e. with so much hard and skilful hypocrisy,
that the husband whom she continually met, and
with whom she was on terms of affection and

confidence, never suspected her, till accident, or the accusation of a third party revealed it to him. What would be the result in such a case? Why that woman would at once forfeit every social right of her existence. She would have no claim on the protection of the law as regarded her children, no claim as regarded her husband, no claim as regarded the slenderest provision that could find her in bread; she would be an outlawed creature; if the husband shut his door against her, and forbade her ever to look on her children again, he would do no more than would be considered justifiable. I am not going here to attack or argue upon the inequality of the law of divorce, in other respects ; but as regards the claim on the children, surely it is a glaring piece of injustice, that while the adulterous wife forfeits every claim of nature, the adulterous husband not only is pronounced fit to fulfil the social relations, as before, but has this ADDITIONAL PRIVILEGE accorded him, that if his wife rebels against his intention of keeping a mistress, he can *punish her for such rebellion,* by wringing from her the only source of happiness she has remaining, in the society and endearments of her infant children !

Such was the case in the instance before us, and such may be the case a hundred times, or a thousand times again, unless some more rational

law be made on the subject. Mrs. Greenhill
tried the Court of Chancery, she tried the Court
of King's Bench, but there was no POWER vested
in either Court to interfere! It may be said
indeed, that since the children were from the
first in the custody of the mother, and were never
surrendered out of that custody, the spirit and
determination shewn by this unhappy young
woman did in fact *baffle the law:* but her case,
as affected by legal decision, is not the less hard.
Mr. Greenhill's object from the beginning was
to prevent proceedings against himself in the
Ecclesiastical Court; *in this he has succeeded.*
His wife, who had not sinned, and who had
already suffered bitterly in consequence of the
discovery of his infidelity, *is compelled by the
effect of the law which obliges her to forfeit her
children, to forego that other law which holds out
to her the slender protection of not being legally
bound to live with her husband;* she is either to
be an exile abroad, or *by law* a prisoner in England for such term as she may have incurred by
contempt of Court; and the husband is to have
the triumph of finding, that not only there is no
punishment for HIS *adultery,* but that the state
of the law as regards his offspring, does in fact
hold out a *protection* to him; and supplies him
with a power over his wife, of which he himself
was probably not aware, when he first sent Mr.

B. to Exeter with conditional offers of arrangement and separate maintenance.

To counterbalance so much of evil, there should
exist in this law some great and necessary good;
some good which cannot be achieved *but* by the
carrying into effect these arbitrary regulations; I
hope, in the general observations which follow
the cases, to prove that no such good results from
it, but on the contrary that it is in every way
productive of mischief.   I shall be happy to meet
the arguments of any one who will attempt to
prove the contrary and to defend the law in its
present state, and meanwhile I leave the case of
Mrs. Greenhill, as one, which while it makes all
future attempts on the part of women LEGALLY to
retain their children a MOCKERY, affords, as I
think, the strongest proof in the world that the
absolute right of the father should not exist.   In
it, and in support of it, were quoted all the previous cases I have given, each of which is an
aggravated instance of injustice; and from it may
be drawn a deduction injurious to the best interests of society, since it teaches women rather to
depend, as they are already prone to do, on wild
and romantic expedients, than on the protection
afforded them by the laws and rules which govern
that society.

It is impossible to find fault with the conduct
of Mrs. Greenhill, in withdrawing herself and
little ones, after the decision given; since that

decision was to leave her in the bloom of youth deceived, betrayed, and utterly desolate, while it sent her children to glean what affection their father could spare, from the fiercer fire of an illicit attachment; perhaps to share that affection with a spurious offspring. It is not my object, nor is it necessary, to argue how far treachery and profligacy in a man may be said to render him an unfit person to educate and train up three daughters in the paths of virtue and peace, but it *is* my object to paint out in the strongest manner the injustice of the non-admission, under such circumstances, of " the Mother's Natural Claim."

OBSERVATIONS.

On what principle of *natural* justice the law is
founded, which in cases of separation between
husband and wife, throws the whole power of
limiting the access of a woman to her children
into the hands of her husband, it is difficult to
say. A man should hardly be allowed to be ac-
cuser and judge in his own case, and yet such is
the anomalous position created by the law.
Whatever be the *cause* of separation, whether in-
compatibility of temper, or imputation of graver
offence, the feelings on both sides must be very
bitter, bitter almost to desperation, before the parties can consent to publish their quarrel to the
world, and break through ties voluntarily formed
and cemented by holy vows. The husband who
contemplates such a separation, is certainly angry,
probably mortified, and in nine cases out of ten,
eager to avenge his real or fancied injuries. To
this angry man, to this mortified man, the law
awards that which can rarely be entrusted to any
human being, even in the calmest hours of life,
namely, DESPOTIC POWER ; while to the woman,
however wronged, however innocent, it is not
even granted to appeal from the tyranny which
oppresses her.

Doubtless the claim of a father is sacred and
indisputable, but when the mother's claim clashes
with it, surely *something* should be accorded to

her. There are other laws besides those made by men—what says the holier law, the law of nature?

Does *nature* say that the woman, who endures for nearly a year a tedious suffering, ending in an agony which perils her life, has no claim to the children she bears? Does *nature* say that the woman, who after that year of suffering is over, provides from her own bosom the nourishment which preserves the very existence of her offspring, has no claim to the children she has nursed? Does *nature* say that the woman who has watched patiently through the very many feverish and anxious nights which occur even in the healthiest infancy, has no claim to the children she has tended? And that the whole and sole claim rests with him, who has slept while she watched; whose knowledge of her sufferings is confined to the intelligence that he is a father; and whose love is *at best* but a reflected shadow of that which fills her heart? No! the voice of nature cries out against the inhuman cruelty of such a separation.

It has been asserted that the instances are very rare in which a man will utterly deprive a mother of her children, and that it is irrational to expect the law to be altered to meet these few instances, considering the difficulties attending such an alteration. Without arguing at present why it should be *more* difficult to make the rule in the case of legitimate children, than in the case of bastards, it may reasonably be asked, are not *all* instances of social wrong *comparatively few* in great social bodies? Parricide is the least frequent of crimes ; yet there is a law against it, and a punishment provided for the criminal. If the law *be,* indeed, to protect the weak against the strong, surely, even for those few cases, some protection should be found. Most undoubtedly, there are many men whose sense of justice, affection for their children, and perhaps some lingering tenderness for the woman herself, would prompt to a merciful consideration of her feelings; but there are others whose hearts are harder, who sacrifice all to the indulgence of an unmanly vengeance, and who, with natures not fine enough for mercy, do (to use the expressive language of Scripture) " *seethe the kid in its mother's milk ;*" punish the child in a spirit of retaliation upon the woman, and involve the innocent and helpless in the suffering consequent upon disputes which they are not even able to understand.

If it be said, that in cases where husband and wife separate, both parents being equally attached to the children, it would be an equal injustice to take them from the father's custody, in order to place them in that of the mother ; I answer, that at the tender age of which alone I speak, they are not, and *necessarily cannot be,* in the custody of the father. The daily tenderness, the watchful care, the thousand offices of love, which infancy requires, cannot be supplied by *any* father, however vigilant or affectionate. The occupations of his life would alone prevent his fulfilling the petty cares which surround the cradle. He is compelled to find *other* care for them, to replace that of which he has deprived them; he is compelled either to leave them to hired female servants, or to deliver them over to some female relative. And it is in this very point that Nature speaks for the *mother*. It pronounces the protection of the father insufficient,—it pronounces the estrangement from the mother *dangerous and unnatural*, and such as must be immediately supplied by female guidance of some sort or other. Does not this, of itself, demonstrate the harsh and unjust tenor of the law? Why should the father, whose utmost care is *insufficient* for the care of his infant children, have power to take them from the mother, whose care *is* sufficient? The question evidently is not whether they shall be taken from the *father*, to be given to the *mother*; the question is, whether they shall be taken from the *mother* to be given to A STRANGER. In no one of the instances by which this work is illustrated, were the children ACTUALLY in the father's custody. De Manneville was obliged to give his infant to a nurse; McClellan and Ball sent theirs to a schoolmistress, Skinner gave his to the woman with whom he cohabited; and Mr. Greenhill intended his mother to take charge of his children. I say that no such law should exist

as that which permits such an abuse of natural
rights. That if it be necessary for the adminis-
tration of hereditary property, and the preservation of the due authority of a husband, that his
right as a father should be *nearly* absolute, there
should at least be so much *real* equality in the
apparently equal claim of both parents,—that he
should be compelled to assign a sufficient cause
for such a separation to the courts of law, and
that if it appear there is *no* just and sufficient
cause, it should not be in the power of any human
being violently to wrest from her a charge appointed her, not by MAN, but by GOD; a charge
which no other can adequately fulfil, and in depriving her of which a serious injury is done to
the children. I say, that till a child is seven
years old, NO cause should enable the father to
take it from the mother, except INSANITY and
PROVED ADULTERY.

It is a rash thing of any man to assert that it
is *not* an injury done to his children thus to deprive them of the careful affection which should
have guarded their early years. He who imagines
he can find a *substitute* for maternal affection has
never felt its full value; he who can consent from
anger and caprice to wean his children from *their*
mother, has never truly loved and respected his
own. How many worthy and celebrated men
have asserted that they owed all they were to that
earliest and holiest guidance? How many men

who have passed a dissipated and profligate youth, have declared that the first impressions given in childhood returned to them afterwards, and that the precepts which cheered their declining lives, were those which a MOTHER's voice repeated to them in infancy ?

It *is* an injury : one of which he cannot foresee the nature or extent. To say nothing of the superior knowledge of an infant's temper and constitution which the mother must have, who has watched it from the day of its birth, I will merely urge that there is no surer receipt for destroying the disposition of any human being than to place him in a false and unnatural position ; and what can be more false and unnatural than the position of children, who, with two parents living, are given over to hired care, or the custody of strangers, *knowing that they* HAVE *a mother*, whom they are neither taught to love, nor permitted to see? They may, I grant, be as well fed, as strictly watched, as diligently instructed, but when all is done which can be done, there will still be something wanting : the halo of a mother's love will be missed from the barren years of their infancy ; they who were little loved, may be supposed to love little in return ; that anomalous infancy may recoil on the father himself, and the children, of whom he kept *forcible* possession in his youth, may turn from him in his old age.

Let us argue it another way. Suppose that these unhappy women had *voluntarily* withdrawn from the task assigned them, what would be said? Suppose that Mrs. de Manneville had abandoned her baby in the cradle; that Mrs. McClellan had left her diseased and dying child to suffer and depend on the care and compassion of strangers; that Mrs. Greenhill had *forsaken* those little children whose tender years required all her attention; what would be said in such a case? Would not the mothers (*even though* THE FATHER *remained in charge of his offspring*) be stigmatised as monsters? Would not the forlorn situation of the children excite compassion in every heart? Would not the words " motherless" and " deserted," imply a foul wrong done to those infants, and an unnatural callousness of heart in the woman who had so abandoned her trust? Most assuredly they would; and why? *Because a mother's love is believed to be the strongest tie of nature, and* HER CARE TO BE ESSENTIAL TO THE WELL-BEING OF HER INFANT CHILDREN. In the beautiful imaginary appeal to the seducer, spoken by Curran, when arguing a famous case;* he calls the abandonment of the child "THAT MOST DEPLORABLE OF HUMAN CONDITIONS, *the orphanage which springs not from the grave, which falls not from the hand of Providence or the stroke of death,* but *comes, before its time; anticipated and inflicted by the* REMORSELESS CRUELTY

* Massey *v.* Headfort.

of parental guilt." Here is admitted, to the fullest extent, the evil done to the infant, and the suffering which such a parting *ought* to inflict on the mother; it ought, according to our ideas of human feeling, TO BE IMPOSSIBLE that a woman should *voluntarily* forego this claim. Why then—*why* then, I ask, does the *reverse* of the case make the injury done seem so light,—the suffering endured so little to be regarded? If the children *are* forlorn and injured by the separation, they are not *less* forlorn or *less* injured, because that separation was not a willing one; if it be *indeed* so unnatural in the mother to *leave* them, is it natural in the father to tear them from her?

It is *not* a natural or just thing for any man to do: it is a thing to weigh and consider; a thing for which he is accountable to those very infants when they shall hereafter ask him, *why, with a living mother*, THEY *were made orphans;* a thing for which he *ought* to be accountable to his country's law.

But even admitting (which I do not) that as far as the children are concerned, no injury or suffering need result from the exertion of " the father's right;" admitting that some near relative undertakes the charge, and fulfils it with tenderness and truth; or admitting, (which rarely happens) that the infants remain under the father's roof, and that he personally superintends the arrangements made for their comfort and happiness ;— still there remains the suffering inflicted on the mother.

There are few men who would stand tamely by and see a woman *struck*, even by her husband ; there are few men, who, even in a common street row, would not interfere to protect the wretched drunken creature whose coarse abuse has provoked the blows of her brutal partner ; yet what degree of bodily agony, or bodily fear, can compare with the inch-by-inch torture of this unnatural separation ? What pain would the mother not thankfully take in exchange for *that* feeling, which remained without a name till an accomplished scholar and gentleman* beautifully phrased it,

" The mighty *hunger of the heart !*"

Yet from this unendurable agony—this legalized torture, there is no protection to be found, nor any arm that can ward off the blow.

Of the extent of the torture felt, no *man* is perhaps an adequate judge, or there might be found still fewer (nominally Christians and gentlemen) who would inflict it. Yet one would think that it required but very little imagination to conceive the effect on a woman's heart, of suddenly snapping the tenderest of ties, and depriving her of the sweetest and most continual of occupations : that without drawing on a morbid fancy for a strained

---

* Sergeant Talfourd in his tragedy of Ion.

and exaggerated picture of distress, there must
be something very dreary in the silence of her day;
something very bitter in the perpetual recurrence
of the hour devoted for years to her good-night
visit to her nursery ; something very *wearing* in
the nights of fitful sleep, disturbed by the indis-
tinct, yet heavy consciousness of sorrow; something very maddening in the bursts of intense
longing to be *with* her children—to know how
they are treated ;—to guard, to guide ;—to be in
short what a mother's love *is*, an INFERIOR PRO-
VIDENCE over those beloved and helpless creatures !   And this is a grief which does not wear
out or go by like other sorrows ;—it is the
torture of a lifetime.   Why should *any* man
have power, because *he* is offended, to inflict the
torture of a lifetime ? It does not necessarily follow because this woman has quarrelled with *him*,
that she must be in the wrong ; on the contrary,
it may be obvious to the whole world that she is
not in the wrong, the wrong may (as in Mrs.
Greenhill's case) be notoriously and confessedly
on *his* side, and even those who publicly award
the custody of the child to the father may admit
that she suffers most unjustly.   Why *should* she
suffer unjustly ?   Because it is so written in the
law?   There is a story of Shylock, and *the pound
of flesh nearest the heart of his victim*, which might
bear some analogy to cases like these.

And here I cannot help recurring to an obser-

vation already made in these pages, namely, the
fact, that on various occasions both Counsel and
Judge have expressed in the clearest manner their
opinion upon the harsh and unnatural effect of
the law, and it has been constantly urged in Court
that if the mothers of BASTARD infants are protected from this misery, *a fortiori* the mothers of
LEGITIMATE children should also be protected.
Now what is there so immutable in this "common
law right of the father," that it should *force men to
decide against their feelings of natural justice?* Is
this abuse to exist *for ever*, because it was not at
first perceived ? or are we waiting till some fright-
ful catastrophe—some violence of a woman driven
to desperation, shall afford an excuse for discussing the nature of the decisions which are well
calculated to cause such results ?—till some second
Mde. de Manneville shall bring herself to the
gallows by a frenzied stab at the man who is
wresting her infant from the breast, and those
who are compelled to admit her *sentence* just, yet
think the previous suffering too oppressive for
human nature to bear? That law is allowed to be
a dangerous and defective one, of which the *severity*
is so much more apparent than the *equity*, that
men rather side with the sufferer, than approve
the punishment ; and for this reason where there
is a permitted discretion, that discretion is exerted
in favour of those who have received unendurable
provocation. It is not very long since a woman

was proved to have stabbed a man with an oyster knife, with such force, that she could not withdraw the knife from the wound. It was urged for her, and *successfully* urged, that she had received from this man an insult which " FEMALE MODESTY" could not brook. Is maternal instinct *weaker*, then, than female modesty? Far from it! God, for the preservation of universal life, made it the strongest of natural instincts. It will make the most timid *animal* desperate; and it works not less strongly in the human breast. I know no woman, however gentle, who at the time Mrs. Greenhill's case (assuredly the hardest in which a decision was ever made) was before the public,—did not express herself so *fiercely* as to the nature of that wrong, as to make it marvellous that, considering the many instances in which it has been inflicted, the habits of religious and moral restraint in which women are educated, should have *invariably* proved sufficient to govern even their moments of desperation.

And this brings me to the consideration of another point; namely, whether there is not something in this law calculated to injure the female character, and thereby to militate against the best interests of general society. A woman is expected to perform with the utmost strictness the social duties of life, and much is very justly supposed to depend on the manner in which she fulfils them. Now, is not that a bad law which

gives a right to an angry man, perhaps a vicious
man, to deprive her of the *power* of fulfilling the
first and most sacred duty which devolves to her
in her character of woman ? In the case of Skinner, the man not only was living in adultery, but
*he took his child and placed it under the care of the
woman with whom he was so living,* and the Court
decided that nevertheless he had " the father's
right" to retain possession of it. What must be
the result of thus forcibly and unjustly denying
the mother the natural and holy occupation of
her life ? A woman does not *die* of sorrow, except
in rare instances ; neither does she become insane,
except in rare instances, where vexation acts on
a naturally nervous and exciteable temperament.
She *exists ;* with the same warm affections,
the same desire of sympathy, the same necessity for exercising those sympathies as before:
she has no share or portion in the cares of public
life ; *every occupation of her existence is more or
less dependent on* THE AFFECTIONS. What then ?
because a man has mercilessly taken from her the
legitimate objects of those affections, is it certain,
is it even *probable,* that they will never again be
exercised ?—Is not the restlessness of the human
heart proverbial ? Do we not *all* endeavour to
satisfy its restlessness by clinging to particular
interests and particular preferences ? Assuredly
we do, and so will it be in the case of this woman
in her unnatural and anomalous position—a wife,

but alone ;—a mother, but without her children.
Shall it be said a man is not responsible for
this? That if she seek her consolation in hollow
gaiety, or unlawful affection, he who has driven
her from that narrow but complete circle, where
she would thankfully have remained ;—he, who
has made the natural exercise of her heart's best
feelings *impossible,* has nothing to answer for? I
say he *has:* and that the law which permits this
ill-exercised responsibility holds out an incentive
to SIN.

I know there is one great answer to the suppo-
sition of this state of feeling on the part of
the woman; namely, that if she be indeed worthy,
and suffering unjustly, she ought to find her rest
neither in human love nor frivolous pleasure, but
in God.

" Beyond the clouds !—beyond the storm !"

To that answer there is no argument of reply.
SHE OUGHT. It is granted. But the frailty of
human nature shews us that instances of perfectly pious resignation are rare; and there
is perhaps no moment of life in which it is more
difficult to feel religiously than while we are
smarting under the injustice of man ; the injustice is so real, so actual, so oppressive; the Eternal
justice which permits that partial wrong for
unknown purposes appears so vague and far !
The law acts *for the multitude,* and among the

multitude there are few unfortunately who would not either catch at such consolation as the world could offer, or take their sorrow like the Rachel of Scripture, who, in spite of these and other reflections, remained " *weeping for her children, and would not be comforted, because* THEY *were not!*"

Again, it is an immoral law as regards *the man*, for men are apt to be careless of such crimes as bring neither disgrace by their detection, nor penalty by their commission. The tone of society is already lax enough, without holding out this direct assurance that the lawgivers and authorities of the realm do not consider a man the worse father of a family because he is an adulterer. Many a man might be checked and restrained from the indulgence of a vicious inclination by the thought that such indulgence would break up his domestic circle, and while it gave his wife a right to withdraw from him, gave *him* no power to torture her into acquiescence or submission, by detaining her children.

It is also a law involving an evident inconsistency, if we consider it relatively to a woman's social position in other respects.

In the matter of marriage, a girl even of fifteen or sixteen is held to be a capable and responsible being, able to make a choice, to decide on her future destiny, and to bind herself by a voluntary oath to the husband she has chosen. Does she *cease* to be a capable and responsible being after her marriage, that in the matter of Maternal Right she is no more considered than a stock or a stone? Is she, whose responsibility in early youth was so great that the rashness of an hour could bind her for life, transformed in her maturer years into an automaton to be moved only at the will of others? Is she, who was so all-important as a bride, *nothing* as a mother? One would imagine the very reverse should be the case, unless indeed the laws be made for *men* alone, and the sole reason of such contradictory regulations be, that it would interfere with the passions of men that these young girls should not have the power to give themselves away while infants by the law;—it would interfere with the passions of men that these young girls in after years should have a distinct and separate claim to those who are infants in very fact and truth.

Yet surely, *surely* this should not be! A man does not purchase a wife as he would buy a fine blood-mare, or a hound, to continue a race of animals and then be got rid of, her offspring remaining his undoubted and undisputed property. He chooses a companion; a thinking, acting, reflecting being; one, who, if a mother, is the mother of immortal souls, and accountable to God for the trust. That man may afterwards repent the choice he made and become discontented with it, but his discontent does not transform the woman into a cipher or a slave: it does not re-

verse and alter every right and purpose of her
existence : it does not, or rather it *ought not*, to
change her from a wife and mother into a thing
as helpless, useless, and blighted, as a scathed
tree. She can make no other choice ; she can
form no other tie ; it is a sin if she even allow her
secret heart to wander to another object ; SHE belongs (parted though she be) to *him* and to his
children :—Do neither then belong to *her?*

But it is said, (and this embraces the commonest
and most urgent objection made to the admission
of the mother's claim to the custody of her children ;) that such a claim *may interfere with
their pecuniary interests;* that a bequest made
by relations,or even the inheritance of the father,
may be affected by it ; and a supposed case has
been put to me by way of illustration, namely,
that property shall be left to a child or children,
on condition they are taken out of the mother's
hands—that the mother persists in keeping them ;
that she does so for a year or two years, and then
dies, leaving the children still infants ; and it is
asked, would not the children very justly complain of the hardship of their being so deprived
of a great benefit, merely because while they were
yet too young to make their own election, or com-
prehend their true interests, they were kept for a
little while by the mother, in defiance of a rich
relation ? I think they *would* complain justly,
but not of the mother, who acted according to

F

the dictates of nature, but of those persons who endeavoured to make a condition *against* nature.

What would be thought of a man who should come to his nephew, and say, " I perceive that you and your father frequently dispute, and that you are not on the best terms with him; I hear also that you are in embarrassed circumstances, and that money is doubly an object to you as you have a large family for whom you are unable to provide; now I will make a proposal to you:— I never liked your father, and would be glad to do him an ill turn; if you will promise to cut him, and never again to enter his house or go near him, I will pay your debts—settle something handsome on you, and make your children my heirs." Would not the man to whom such a proposal was made, resent it as an insult, or consider it as a mark of insanity on the part of the proposer? And yet it is not one whit *more* ridiculous, or *more* unjust, to propose to the son to hold no communication with his father for the sake of a bequest, than to propose that a child shall have no communication with its mother, on the same conditions; nor do the terms in which the proposal is made, materially differ, being in effect as follows : "Come, you and your wife quarrel a good deal, and you are very poor; you know we all thought your marriage a folly, and never could endure the woman; get rid of her, and promise us that she never shall see her children again;

and we will make your circumstances easy, and
provide satisfactorily for your little boys." I repeat that it is a condition against nature ; and
perhaps the best and simplest answer to the objection urged, is, that *if that condition were ren-
dered impossible by law, it would not be made,* and
consequently COULD NOT interfere with the pecuniary interests of the children, as it is likely to
do at present. If it were once settled that every
mother had *a right* to the care of an infant of
tender age, and that afterwards she had a right
of access to them, no man would *propose* to an
angry husband to disgrace the best feelings of his
nature by entering into a covenant with others, to
oppress and torture a woman for a certain advantage to be obtained for himself and children : and
it may be doubted whether people would not continue to leave legacies to their near relations, just
as often and as readily as when they could *buy
and sell the mother's claim* to gratify a feeling of
aversion or revenge.

The same reasoning might apply to the sup-
position of the father himself refusing to leave
his property to children brought up by a mother
with whom he had quarrelled : with this additional argument, that the father who for so harsh
and capricious a reason would injure a child's
prospects, would have been equally likely to dis-
inherit his offspring for any other cause, though
that cause were never so groundless. There is

ample time *after* the child shall have passed the age of nurture, to place it under the care of those whose peculiar system of education may best suit the father's views, therefore it cannot be from disapproval of the child, but from hatred to the mother, that the threat of disinheritance is held out.

No one will say that a child of seven years of age has formed *opinions*, the father can instil what opinions he pleases. The *disposition* of the child *is* probably formed, the guidance of which would probably, under the father's roof, have been left to a servant, instead of the tender and watchful care of a mother; but all the rest is still in the father's power, and is, in fact, all that *should* belong to the father's right; nor is it possible to conceive a rational being saying, " Because this child *lived with the mother till seven years of age,* it shall never inherit my property."

Another specious plausibility on the part of those who would defend the separation of mother and child, is this, that a man may feel his wife to be a very unfit person to educate his children, and may even feel convinced that she has been guilty of sin, without being able legally to prove it, or even to make it evident to the world.

I confess that I am exceedingly sceptical as to the last assertion; since it is rare that if crime is *committed*, it cannot also be *proved*. But admitting, for the sake of argument, that such *might* be the case in isolated instances, even *then*, IN DEFAULT OF PROOF, I say the woman should retain her infant child. The misconduct of the husband is reckoned as nothing; though glaring and offensive, *his* adultery bars no claim, unless it can be proved that *the child is brought into contact with* THE MISTRESS *so as to be corrupted.* The *corruption of the child* is then the only point considered by the law. Now that supposed lightness of behaviour in a woman, which cannot be proved, which is not evident to her family or the world, and which is merely asserted by her husband, who admits that he CANNOT *make it evident*, is not *very* likely to corrupt, or be obvious to, a child under seven years of age; and if it be persisted that even at *that* tender age, a want of principle can be instilled by example, or caused by want of holy precept, we will grant also *that* for the sake of argument; and *having* granted it, ask, why, in God's name, *if the child can be corrupted by the existence of the principles which cause the misconduct of the* MOTHER (though the misconduct itself be *not* evident), is it safe from the influence of the principles of the FATHER merely because it does not see or consort with his mistress? The mistress may not be so bad as he; she may have broken no marriage tie to live with him, why is *hers* the only corrupting power, when his is an equal or greater dereliction from moral principle?

It is also urged that a man may consider his wife to be of too weak an understanding, or too uncertain a temper, to educate her infant child, and that it would be a strange exertion of power on the part of the law to compel him under such circumstances to leave it in her hands. But if he had not quarrelled with his wife, and the two parents had continued to live together, that woman, however foolish and capricious, would have exercised the rights and privileges of a mother under his roof, nor would he probably have thought it necessary, *while the child was within the age of nurture,* even to call in the aid of a governess, far less to send it from its natural home to be brought up by strangers. It is to be regretted that he made so bad a choice of the person who was to be the partner of his life, and the mother of his children, but he is not therefore to acquire a right to exile that woman from all the interests of her life. There is scarcely any mother who is not both *able and anxious* to train up her *infant* child, (or if there be such, they are not likely to dispute the possession of their children), and, after that child has ceased to be an infant, the father is at liberty to exert his parental authority, so far as may be necessary in his eyes, for its welfare and instruction.

I have already earnestly deprecated the idea that I would set up the claim of the mother *in opposition* to that of the father; on the contrary, I desire to unite these claims as far as is con-

sistent with the unhappy position of a separation
between man and wife. I would have the mother's claim *conditionally* admitted, as for instance,
that where (as in Mrs. Greenhill's and Mrs.
Ball's case) a man was living in adultery, and
refused to part with his mistress, he should not
be able to *take his children from the mother*, even
though on account of his adultery she separated
herself from him, and though they should be *past*
the age of nurture. That in all cases where
access was to be forbidden, a man should be compelled to assign a rational cause for the cruel
separation he desired to inflict, and answer the
mother's appeal in the Court of Chancery : and
that it should not be LEGAL for any man to seize
and convey away children under the age of nurture
and conceal them from the mother, as in the case
of Mrs. de Manneville and Mrs. Norton.

It would have been an easier and less invidious
task, to have written on the subject *generally*,
and without reference to the several parties whose
names are here brought forward ; but I have
considered that by so doing I might fail of bringing the hardship endured so forcibly home to my
readers. It was well and truly remarked by one
whom I have already quoted, and who was, perhaps, the most eloquent pleader that ever lived, *
that to ensure men's sympathy for a great general
wrong shared by hundreds, it was best to de-

* Curran—Heevy *v.* Sirr.

scribe a *single* example of suffering; since otherwise "*nothing defined or specific finds its way to the
heart, nor is any sentiment excited save that of a
general erratic unappropriated commiseration.*" I
have given *six* distinct cases of wrong, each of
which presents (under different features) a common resemblance.

In the cases of De Manneville and M'Clellan
no accusation was made against the mother, and
no reason given for withholding the custody of the
infant from her.

In the cases of Skinner, Ball, and Greenhill,
not only was no accusation made against the mother, but the father was living in open adultery.

In the case of Smith (quoted by the Vice-
Chancellor in that of Ball), no accusation was
made against the mother, but on the contrary it
was proved that the father took the children as a
measure of annoyance, to force the mother to relinquish some property settled separately on her.

In all these cases, and in others which I
have omitted, it has been always urged for the
woman, that there existed no reason *why* her
children should be cruelly taken from her; and
a great deal of vain eloquence and argument has
been expended in her behalf. To that eloquence
and to those arguments I have found but one
reiterated reply—"It is THE LAW," "It is so
written in the bond." I have not found one reason, or one attempt to assign a reason, for the

meditated or enforced separation, but only—" It is the law."

Now, if the cruelty, hardship, aye, and *injustice* of the pain inflicted, be acknowledged even by those whose province it is to *administer* the law ; if a Judge and Vice-Chancellor in giving his decision, observed, that he would gladly adopt any precedent of authority for mercy, *because in a* MORAL *point of view he knew of* NO *act more harsh and cruel than depriving the mother of proper intercourse with her child:*—if it is only THE LAW which stands against the admission of the mother's natural claim—what hinders that the law be altered?

Surely in this country, where hatred of all oppression is made a national boast, where if a man were to strike his little footboy, an action would lie for assault and damages—where even offensive and violent language subjects a man to a penalty ; in this country, and at this time, when all liberal opinions are encouraged and fostered, it is a strange and crying shame, that the only despotic right an Englishman possesses is to wrong the mother of his children! That compelled as he is by the equal and glorious laws of his nation, to govern even the *words in which his anger is expressed* to his fellow men and subjects, he may act what cruelty he pleases by his own fire-side, and he who dares not in the open street lay a finger on the meanest man there, may stand on his own hearth and tear from the very breast of the nursing mother, the little unconscious infant whose lips were drawing from her bosom the nourishment of life!

Is this the vaunted justice—the vaunted mercy of the English code? Shall it be said that there is in England a legal protection for *every* right and *every* claim, natural and artificial, except ONE; and *that* ONE is the tie between mother and child! Over *that* there is no protection; in support of *that* the courts " have no *power* to interfere;" in making laws for the human race, the mothers of the human race were forgotten! They were *forgotten;* that is the word. There is no positive enactment that for any crime she can commit against the law, a woman's infant children shall be torn from her; but there is a negative rule, that if they *are,* by the father, taken from her, the law cannot compel restitution.

Now, I think, that there should be an *active power to protect* vested in the law in this instance, as in all others.

The law is absurd and unnatural which orders a guiltless and unoffending woman to deliver up her children to a man who braves all decency by living with a paramour, when, *were the case reversed,* he might turn his wife into the streets, and forbid her to behold them!

The law is absurd and unnatural which leaves *my* woman so utterly at the mercy of a man, who, if he be guilty of no *other* fault towards her, must have a heart of stone to enable him to resist the representations of misery and distress on the part of one whom he formerly professed to love, and whose fondness for the children of whom he deprives her, he has had a daily opportunity of witnessing.

Lord Denman said, in Mrs. Greenhill's case, "I think it right to act *on the general rule.* No doubt ought to exist in the public mind on this subject. A decision on a particular state of facts alone, might raise a doubt as to whom the custody of the children ought to belong; might lead to the greatest family discord; and might thus endanger the lives of the most helpless part of mankind." The wisdom of this brief explanation as to the necessity of a GENERAL RULE, cannot for a moment be disputed. It is obvious to the most simple, that every law must be based on some broad principle, from which principle the minor circumstances varying every separate case shall have no power to make the judge depart; and on the plea of this allowed necessity much severity is excused, and much painful sympathy is overcome. But the question here, is not whether it is requisite *to establish and act upon a* GENERAL RULE, but whether *that* GENERAL RULE *should be the one now followed*, or whether a BETTER general rule might not be substituted in its place.

Lord Erskine, when first at the bar, is reported
to have said to a Judge, who, in contradicting
his argument, made use of the somewhat con-
temptuous expression, " Such was the law before
you were born :" "*It is because I was not born
that it was the law, and I will see it altered before
I die.*" Is there not *one* of all who acted as
counsel or judge in the cases I have given, who
will say the same of this ? The real question (as
was briefly and eloquently said in Mrs. Greenhill's
case) is, "*whether the* RIGHT OF THE FATHER
amounts to the EXCLUSION OF THE MOTHER ?" If
it does *not* amount to such exclusion, then some
alteration is imperatively necessary ; and I think
there will hardly be found a man bold enough
to assert, in the face of these cases, that a father
should have this UNLIMITED POWER TO EXCLUDE
THE MOTHER WITHOUT CAUSE. The man who
does assert it, avows his readiness, on the first occasion of quarrel, to tear *his* infants from their
mother ; there is no medium ; either he thinks
the power should exist TO BE EXERTED, or that it
should not exist at all.

The days are fortunately gone by when a
dogged opposition to all change, checked every
step towards improvement in our institutions.
Laws are constantly revised ; many even while
nominally existent, have fallen into disuetude ;
and since it has been shewn that *no* crimi-
nality on the part of the husband, nor innocence

on the part of the wife, can influence the decisions
made, either in the Court of King's Bench,
or the Court of Chancery: that apparently,
while the law stands as it does, these Courts have
no option in their decisions; it is surely high
time that some alteration should be made which
would enable them to exercise a discretion in cases
like these.

I am told that the difficulty is, to meet every
individual instance of alleged hardship, and to
enter into private complaints and family disputes,
as must necessarily be the case if the Court is
called upon to decide the right of access of the
mother against the inclination of the father.
But it is notorious that both the Court of King's
Bench and the Court of Chancery do ALREADY
assume to themselves *some* power of meeting and
deciding on individual cases. They will interfere for the security of property, and on account
of religious, or even political opinions ; and have
established a rule that *at a specified age*, namely,
14 years, a child cannot be forced back to the custody of its father, *if the child himself be unwilling
so to return*, as in the case of the King *v.* Pene-
lope Smith,* where a father having sued the
Court of King's Bench for a writ of habeas corpus, in order to obtain possession of his son (a
boy between 13 and 14), from an aunt who kept
him ; the Court REFUSED TO DETERMINE *the*

* 2 Str. 982.

right of guardianship, but set the child at liberty, telling him he might go where he thought fit : on the principle that WHERE THE CHILD IS OF AN AGE TO JUDGE FOR ITSELF, *the Court will not deliver it into the custody of the father.* But, indeed, the very fact of the claims of Mrs. Greenhill and others having been ARGUED IN COURT, proves at once both the power vested in the Court to *meet* and weigh the circumstances of individual cases, and the assumption of a doubt as to which *parent* the custody of the children would eventually be awarded. It therefore becomes a simple question whether the Courts (*having* assumed the power to decide), REFUSE TO CONSIDER the three points submitted as proper to influence their decisions, namely, the suffering of the mother, the injury done to the child, and the immoral tendency of the present state of the law.

The suffering of the mother admits of neither argument nor doubt. The immoral tendency of a law which allows the man to sin with impunity, and leaves the woman deprived of the holiest, and most virtuous occupation of her life, has, I think, been shewn : and the injury done to the child is sufficiently obvious (even without the reasoning adduced at a former page), in the fact that the father is not obliged to prove that the custody in which he places the child is equally advantageous to that child's health or moral improvement, as if it had remained with his wife ; nor is he

obliged to shew that his sister, mother, or whatever female guardian he may appoint, has quali-
ties which make her more fit for the exercise of
responsible power, and better able to educate his
child than the mother from whom it is taken.
He is in no way accountable for the disposal of
his trust (as indeed was proved in the wretched
case of the man Skinner and his mistress Anne
Deverall). There is no consideration as to who
is the best guardian for the child: but the father
exerts a right over the custody of its person (which,
be it remembered, is almost invariably a *nominal*
and not a *bona fide* custody), *not necessarily for
the advantage of the infant,* but because the law
awards it to him as a GENERAL RULE ; by which
rule the child's morals may or may not be injured ;
and its education may or may not be left to ignorant, incapable, and vicious persons.

I have always observed, that to secure attention
to an argument, it is good to put that argument
into plain brief words ; that so, neither the indo-
lent may be wearied, the simple confounded, nor
the proud and ingenious be tempted to prove their
skill by bringing forward all the eloquent plausi-
bilities which exist on the wrong side of a question. Let us then throw aside the technicalities
of law, and consider simply, and in simple words,
what is the NATURE *of the general rule which at
present guides the decisions made in the* PUBLIC
COURTS OF JUSTICE OF A FREE AND CHRISTIAN

COUNTRY, as proved by the recorded cases, *where custody has been* REFUSED, as well as by those in which the father's right has been unconditionally admitted. In simple words then, the rule is this. For its equal justice,—*the father* has a right, and *the child* has a right; the only party who has *no* right is the woman who suffered the peril of that child's birth, and in that hour forgot her sufferings, "*for joy that a man was born into the world.*" For its morality,—*the man living in adultery* has a right, and *the woman living in fornication* has a right, the only party who has NO right, whose claim the law *abjures and denies,* is the wedded mother of a legitimate child!

For its agreement with the general tenor of the laws of the land—the man is amenable to the law as a subject of the king; he is amenable to the law as one of a great social body; he is amenable to the law as a husband; and he is amenable to the law (*as far as the rights of property are concerned*), even as a father. It is only in this single point of the mother's claim that he stands as free and independent of all law as if no such thing existed.

But it is said that the right of the father to his children differs from all others: that the law can scarcely reach it; that it is the RIGHT OF NATURE he exerts, not a power given under the law, and that it is doubtful whether ever such interference as is already assumed, is justifiable. This is a

palpably absurd objection, for it is the right of
nature that a man shall walk abroad, look upon
the sun, and breathe the air of heaven at his pleasure ; it is the first right of his existence ; but
nevertheless, for the protection of others, more or
less related to and connected with him as mem-
bers of the common body, even *that* right is subject to the law ; nor do we consider it an in-
fringement of natural rights, that one who has
offended the law shall be *imprisoned ;* for as
Burke somewhere observes in better words, *man,
in a civilized country, tacitly* AGREES *to exchange*
SOME PORTION *of his natural rights, for the necessary legal protection of the rest.* There is no reason then why a man living under the law should be
independent of it in one single and isolated instance;
nor can the law excuse its non-interference on the
plea of the FATHER's natural right, when it *does*
directly interfere with the natural right of the
MOTHER, and forces her children from her very
breast. Either the right admitted, is NATURAL
or ARTIFICIAL ; if ARTIFICIAL, the law has the
same power to adjudge the custody of infants,
that it would have in case of any other artificial
right ; if NATURAL, the law has no power to order
children from their mother, since by nature the
rights of both parents are co-equal.

I confess, for my own part, I would desire to
see the claim to the custody of children *above
the age of nurture,* at once established among the

artificial rights of the community. I have repeatedly deprecated the notion that I would assert, and endeavour to establish THE MOTHER'S CLAIM, *against the law,* or *in defiance of legal power ;* on the contrary I wish to see that power so firmly established, and so equally exerted, that the woman may *throw herself on its protection, instead of endeavouring to baffle its strength.* I *admit* the right of the father to control the education of his children ; but I do *not* admit his right to sacrifice the interest of their education to personal anger. I *admit* his right to the respect and affection of his offspring; but I do *not* admit his right to deprive the mother of a share of that affection. I *admit* his right, as head of his house, and guardian of his property, to retain them, when parted from the mother, as residents under his own roof, or to choose such place of tuition as may seem best to him ; but I do *not* admit his right to exile the mother from all AC-CESS to her children, to prevent her from gaining intelligence of their welfare, and to inflict upon her the tortures of a life of anxiety and despair.

The question resolves itself into what were best established as a GENERAL RULE; and I think it not unreasonable to expect, that during the tender years of infancy, when the child *cannot even report the treatment it receives at the hands of a stranger,* (in short, while it is under the age of nurture), the general rule should be

the same as in the case of bastard children,
namely, that *it should remain with the mother ;*
and AFTER the age of nurture, that the mother
should not only have a right of access to her
children, but that she should also have a power
of appeal to the Courts, and that the question
should *then* be, whether she was or was not a
preferable guardian to the female relative or governess to whom the father desired to delegate
his authority ; and whether she was or was not
(to say the least) *as* capable of educating them as
the female so proposed. The fact of unfounded
accusations *having been* made, or being *then* made
against her, should not be allowed to bar her
claim, even should those accusations be publicly
advanced in a Court of Justice : for as, already, a
man may desire to divorce his wife in order to
marry his mistress, or to form a union he con-
ceives more advantageous to his interests, or
from vindictive feelings against her; so, in that
case, he might bring forward those accusations
purposely to prevent her being pronounced a fit
person to retain the custody of his children. The
child's real interests, and the woman's actual innocence, should be the points considered ; for, to
quote once more from Curran, " Law cannot *prevent* the envenomed arrow from being pointed at
the intended victim, but it gives him (or her) a
shield in the integrity of a jury." If a woman be
noways guilty, circumstances, according to the

intelligence of the judge, should regulate his decision as to her capability of educating, or degree of access: and in a case like Mrs. Greenhill's, (where not only the breath of slander had never fallen on the mother's name, but the claim on the custody of the children was made *by an adulterous husband, refusing to part with his mistress,*) the infants should remain under the mother's care, and no human being should have power to remove them. This is mere justice; and I perceive in these regulations nothing, as I have before said, which militates *more* against the father's right to educate his children as he shall think fit, than the power already vested in the Court of Chancery; nay, nor *so much;* for that Court *has* assumed to itself a RIGHT OF DECISION how far irreligion and immorality disqualify a man from properly educating his children, or having the custody of them; and though that right has been most sparingly exercised, yet its bare assumption and existence is surely a greater interference with parental power, than if the Court were to assume a right to decide on the mother's claim of access to children above the age of nurture; *her access in no way barring the father's power to bring them up as he pleases.*

Nor do I perceive anything which interferes *more directly* with the general feature of all the laws respecting women, (namely, the non-admission of their separate legal existence when married,) than is the case in *other* instances of protection of their social rights, such as the power vested in the law to guard their property ; to grant a separation *a mensâ et thoro* for cruelty or other causes ; in which the woman's separate existence is acknowledged, and the *husband's power* is *made subordinate to the law.* I consider this a parallel case ; it is a case of simple protection of the liberty and rights of the subject, and not of any encroachment on the authority of a father as the master of the house and the head of his family. The husband, as well as the wife, is amenable to the law in other re-spects—the husband as well as the wife should be amenable in this : nor would fathers themselves be perhaps the *least* grateful for rules which pre-vented their involving themselves in the first hour of anger in a system of unmanly persecution. For it is certain that so dangerous a measure may recoil upon the man who adopts it, as unless (to use the words of the Vice-Chancellor, when quoting the case of Smith *v.* Smith) "*the woman's or the child's* DEATH *determines the question,*"—unless a husband could stab his wife to the heart, and so be rid of her, *her* life will be spent in endeavours to obtain an intercourse with her children, and *his* in struggling to prevent it. The scale may turn either way, and either parent may succeed ; but only *one* can succeed where they are thus opposed : whereas by an adjustment which preserved the mutual rights of *both*, neither would have the temptation to wean the heart of the child from the other. The mother might fulfil the duties appointed her by God, subject to the conditions of education made by the husband ; and the children (who are under the present system most unjustly made sufferers), would enjoy the benefit of the care and affection of *both* parents, and neither lean to the woman, nor imbibe their first notions of religion and humanity from a man, who, whatever his *theory* on the subject may be, *practically* endeavours to teach them the fifth commandment, not as written " Honour your father and mother ;" but according to a reading of his own, " Honour your father and *forget your mother, for she has offended* ME."

And here let me remind my readers, that not only does the state of the law leave to the caprice of an angry man, how far this holy and equal commandment can be obeyed by his children ; but it establishes a principle in direct opposition to religious precept, by treating lightly *that* claim, and *that* affection, which is most strictly and con- tinually urged in Holy Writ. In the book of GOD's law (whatever be its fate by the law of man,) the mother's claim is valued at its worth. There is scarcely a chapter in the inspired writings which does not allude to the tie between mother and child as the strongest of earthly links, and which does not set up the love of a mother beyond all earthly affection. Images of illustration, drawn from the existence of her claim, occur in every page; the Bible teems with them, as the earth, in its spring-time, teems with flowers. The threat of desolation, and the promise of peace, are alike conveyed through the medium of that allegory. The repentant city is told, that *her sons shall come from afar, and her daughters be nursed at her side;* and the curse upon the people of Judah is this : *" let their wives be bereaved of their children."* Allusion is made, not once, or twice, but in hundreds of instances, to the love, the sorrow, and the devotion of a mother. Her sufferings are considered. When the prophet would pourtray the utter defeat and hopeless despair of the men of Edom ; when he desires to convey the strongest image of faint and sinking agony, he says that the hearts of these mighty men *" shall be as the heart of a woman in her pangs."* When the fierce desolation of famine and siege is spoken of, and all the worst horrors which awaited the beleaguered city rise rapidly and crowd upon the mind, one simple thrilling sentence thus comprises what pages of description could scarcely have told : *" The pitiful woman hath sodden her own child !"* The last tie of nature was there forgotten ; so bitter was their misery, so wild their hunger, that the mother—the *pitiful* woman—the fond, yearning, patient mother, found heart to slay her child for food. Other horrors doubtless there were, but none like this ; brutal ferocity was there, and

unprovoked cruelty, and the gnawing death of
starvation endured by hundreds; but all that
could be endured, or inflicted, was weak to that
one terrible image of NATURE'S GREAT INSTINCT
CONQUERED, the "pitiful" woman destroying her
own child.

Nor is it only by illustrations such as these
that the strength and power of that feeling is sha-
dowed forth: there is one sentence of Scripture
which lifts a mother's love from among the passions and affections of human nature, and places
it on a level with that which is Divine. "*Thus
saith* THE LORD: *As one whom his* MOTHER *com-
forteth* SO WILL I COMFORT YOU." Such were the
words by which the Prophet of GOD conveyed to
His creatures the idea of *the perfection of consolation;* such the message which hallowed for ever
that earthly love by its sublime and tender com-
parison!

"There shall be a very bitter mourning," says
the Scripture, in another place, "a mourning as
of a MOTHER for her only son." Shall we, then,
believe the mourning of such is forgotten? No;
"*their tears are before the Lord*"—and his arm is
outstretched to help them. It was in mercy to
this sorrow, that the God of Israel looked down
on banished Hagar, as she sate despairing in the
scorched and trackless desert; and caused a foun-
tain of cool flowing waters to gush from its arid
sands, lest Ishmael should perish in the wil-
derness.

It was in mercy to this sorrow, that the prayer
of the prophet Elisha was heard, in behalf of the
Shunamite; and the breath returned to the corpse
of the little weary one, who, being borne home
fainting from the harvest heat, "lay on his mother's knees till noon, and then died!"

It was in mercy to this sorrow, that the gentle
and compassionate Saviour caused the mourning
procession to pause, at the gates of the city of
Nain, and touched the bier whereon lay the
last remaining hope of a lonely widow; that he
might bid the woman cease from her weeping,
by restoring to her grieving arms the son she
had lost!

But the men who follow that Master—"who
profess and CALL themselves Christians"—deny
the mother's claim, spurn back the mother's
prayer, and see with cold and hardened hearts
the sorrow which melted the compassionate Lord
of Heaven. And when they have condemned the
young children to "the orphanage which springs
not from the grave"—and when, in their cruel
wrath, they have left the woman to that desolation which caused the voice of lamentation to be
heard in Ramah—they yet can bend their steps
to the temple of God; to kneel before Him who
asks "*mercy* and not *sacrifice*;" to repeat the
prayer for the CONDITIONAL forgiveness of tres-
passes; and to bow the head at the name of that
Jesus, whose solemn adjuration called back the

spirit to its forsaken clay, and reversed even the doom of death, to relieve a mother's despair!

I know there are some who will say that this is not a proper place for so solemn an appeal; that I am arguing a point of law, not a religious text, and that I am wandering from the discussion as to whether the uncontrolled right of the father should *exist at all*, to a declamation against the feelings which cause the abuse of that right *as now existing*. But with all submission to those opinions, I must say, I think this *is* the proper place for such an appeal. The law of man was made to ENFORCE, not to SUPERSEDE the law of God: to watch that the divine precepts be obeyed, not to substitute inferior rules in their stead. It is a dangerous doctrine which would utterly separate Human from Divine Law, and which would teach us to consider legislative enactments as independent of, or other than subservient to, the Cause of General Religion. The Scripture says, "He that is not *with* me is *against* me;" and men should beware, lest in denying the necessity of a strict accordance with the spirit of Holy Writ, they fall into the error of making laws in *direct opposition to that spirit*, as surely the present law must be considered. The Roman and the Heathen of old claimed an absolute power over the persons of their children, nay, in some cases over their very lives;—with the gentler creed of more modern days a gentler spirit has crept in, and the laws of a country professing the religion of Christ should preserve at least so much accordance with the precepts of the Founder of that religion, as may suffice to repress the fierce tyranny or unbending harshness which, in the several cases here given, have accompanied the exercise of " The Father's Right."

It is with some reluctance that I now bring to a close the observations I have made, and during the writing of which the fear of being tedious has continually struggled with the fear of not saying all which suggested itself to my mind as likely to convince. I have now done. If I have omitted to answer some argument which might be urged on the contrary side, it is because such argument has not presented itself as probable ; *not* because I have shrunk from meeting it. I have brought to the subject such powers of reasoning as I possess, and such fairness as the human mind can command, under the influence of a strong bias. If it be feebly handled, it has, at least, not been feebly felt : nor am I without sanguine hopes that some one will argue it after me, who will bring to the task a more complete knowledge of technical difficulties which surround the law, and more masculine eloquence to ensure conviction.

There is, in the case of every abuse, and more especially in all instances of defective legislation, an appointed day when men rise up against that which has long been, if not *quietly,* at least *obscurely*

borne,—when the smouldering and consuming
fire bursts into light, and shines like a warning
beacon to the world. It may be that the wrong
done falls at that time on one less able tamely to
submit; or it may be that the last and crowning
example of wrong is one more obvious, palpable,
and revolting than all which have preceded it.
Such I take to be the case in the present instance;
the last case decided under the present law, was
that of Mrs. Greenhill, and I think that when
that young, hapless, unoffending woman was ordered to relinquish her infant children to an
adulterous husband, the law was stamped in
the eyes of all men with cruelty, absurdity, and
injustice.

I will venture to prophecy, that the decision
made in that case, will, sooner or later, *force* a
discussion of the principle on which it was given;
if not for the merits of the case itself, for the in-
calculable mischief it is likely to do. It is, indeed, the crowning example of wrong; it has
shown to all women what their position is in respect of their children: and as it cannot be supposed that *any* lesson will so conquer the instinc-
tive nature of their love, as to make them quietly
surrender their offspring, we may look forward to
the exertion of every species of stratagem and
defiance on the part of those mothers who may
be similarly placed, and who have learned from
that story *to despair of the protection of the law.*

The difficulties attendant upon decisions of a like nature, instead of being *removed* by that unswerving, uncompromising sentence, will be *increased tenfold.* A "general rule," so wholly and utterly opposed to natural justice, will not be borne. Women will copy Mrs. Greenhill's example; they will leave home, they will leave friends, they will leave country, but they will NOT leave *their children;* and a hundred times more confusion and wrong will result than the law will ever put straight again. In that unnatural and revolting strife, the father tearing the child from its mother's breast, the mother flying like a hunted hind, and concealing her little ones from the face of him who should be their natural protector, it *may* perhaps occur to the lawgivers of a free country, that it would be more for the peace of society, and the credit of humanity, conditionally to admit the MOTHER'S NATURAL CLAIM.

THE END.

NORMAN AND SKEEN, PRINTERS, MAIDEN LANE, COVENT GARDEN.

www.ingramcontent.com/pod-product-compliance
Ingram Content Group UK Ltd.
Pitfield, Milton Keynes, MK11 3LW, UK
UKHW042150280225
455719UK00001B/248